HARVARD BEATS YALE 29-29

For Luke
A pleasure to be related.

Cheers,
Kevin Rafferty
NYC 2018

HARVARD BEATS

YALE 29-29

The Story of the Most Famous Football Game Ever Played in the Ivy League . . . as Told by the Players.

Edited by KEVIN RAFFERTY

THE OVERLOOK PRESS
NEW YORK

First published in the United States in 2009 by
The Overlook Press, Peter Mayer Publishers, Inc.

NEW YORK:
141 Wooster Street
New York, NY 10012

Cataloging-in-Publication Data is available from the Library of Congress

Book design and type formatting by Bernard Schleifer
Printed in China
FIRST EDITION
1 3 5 7 9 8 6 4 2
ISBN 978-1-59020-217-3

Harvard Stadium...November 23, 1968

The Vietnam War is raging. Martin Luther King and Robert Kennedy have been assassinated.

For the first time since 1909, the football teams of both Yale and Harvard are undefeated as they meet for their final game.

Yale's quarterback, Brian Dowling, has not lost a game since the 7th grade. Their halfback, Calvin Hill, will be Rookie of the Year playing for the Dallas Cowboys in 1969 and eventually inducted into the NFL Hall of Fame.

Yale, ranked 16th in the nation, is heavily favored. . . .

CONTENTS

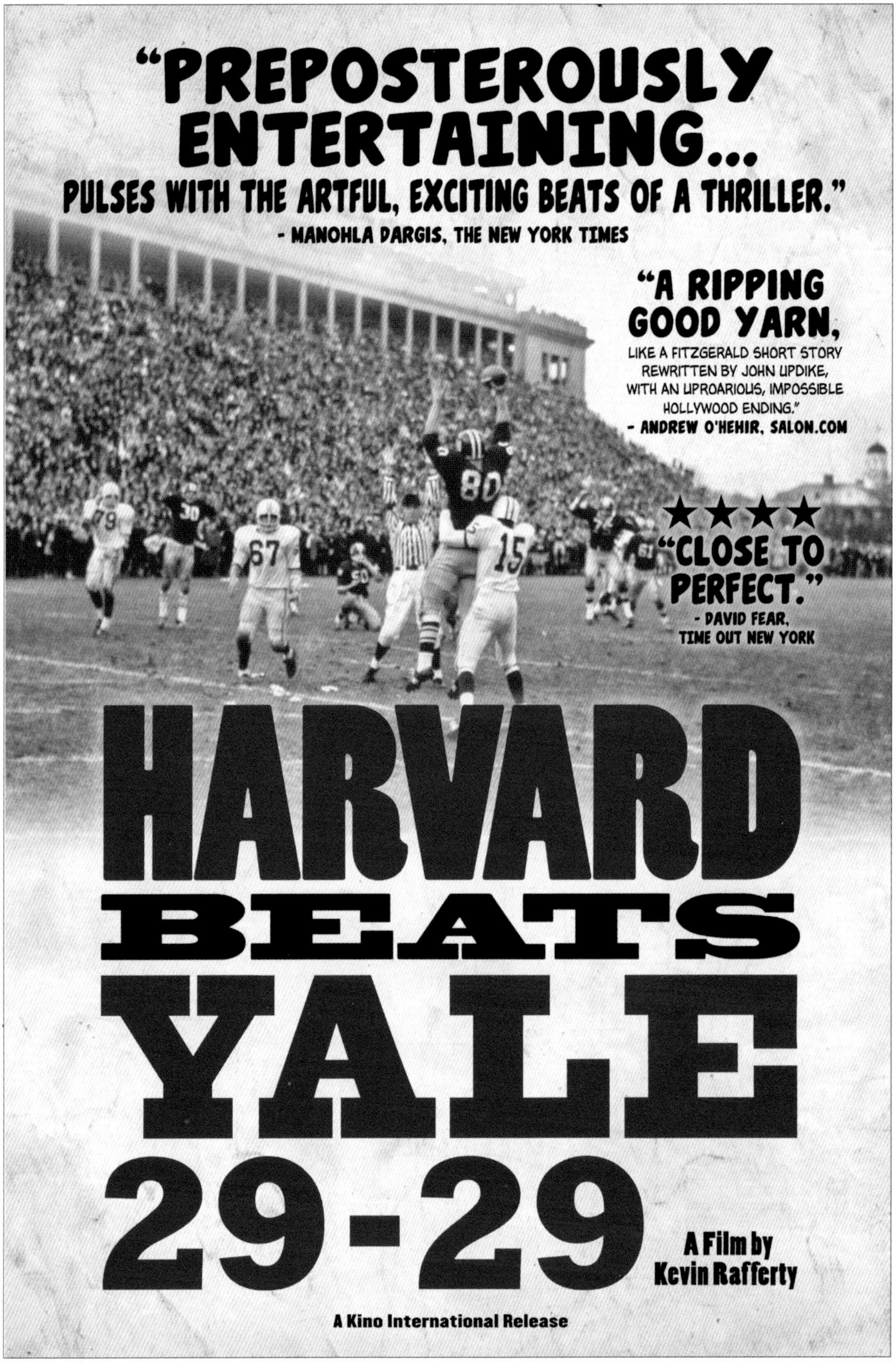

"PREPOSTEROUSLY ENTERTAINING...
PULSES WITH THE ARTFUL, EXCITING BEATS OF A THRILLER."
- MANOHLA DARGIS, THE NEW YORK TIMES
"A RIPPING GOOD YARN,
LIKE A FITZGERALD SHORT STORY REWRITTEN BY JOHN UPDIKE, WITH AN UPROARIOUS, IMPOSSIBLE HOLLYWOOD ENDING."
- ANDREW O'HEHIR, SALON.COM
★★★★
"CLOSE TO PERFECT."
- DAVID FEAR, TIME OUT NEW YORK
HARVARD BEATS YALE 29-29
A Film by Kevin Rafferty
A Kino International Release

INTRODUCTION

This book grew out of a documentary movie that I made, also entitled *Harvard Beats Yale 29-29*. The idea for the movie percolated up from the depths of various aspects of my background.

I went to prep school at Andover for four years where I was in the top fifth of my class for the first year and the bottom fifth thereafter. Don't ask. I was also a bit of a disciplinary problem. I played end on the football team, as had my father (who was captain) and my grandfather (who was captain). I, myself, was not deemed captain material.

Reminders of my family legacy were everywhere. Two of my teachers had taught my father. There was a *Kevin Rafferty Memorial Field*, named after my father's older brother, a fighter-bomber pilot who was shot down and killed by the Nazis in WW2. Once, in a football game, after catching a pass and then having my wind knocked out, I remember the ref leaning down, peering into my helmet and shouting, "Raff? Raff? Is your name Rafferty? I played on your dad's team in 1938!"

In those days Andover was still something of a "feeder" school for Yale, just as our arch-rival Exeter was for Harvard. Forty-two of my Andover classmates went to Yale. A *hundred* of my father's Andover classmates had joined *him* at Yale. My record at Andover did not support a continuation of this tradition. I found out on the day before graduation that I would, indeed, be receiving a high school diploma only as the result of an extremely liberal interpretation of my essay, in the U.S. History final exam, on the Spanish-American War.

I did not get in to Yale. In fact I did not get in to *any* college, including my home state University of Connecticut. So I was sent for a year to a "public" (read private) school in Dorset, England with the hope that I would shape up. There I played on the rugby team, threw the discus farther than anybody else in the West of England, fell in love, lost my virginity, didn't do much academic heavy lifting and generally had a very good time. I applied to colleges again and this time, somehow, got in to Yale, Harvard and Columbia.

All of which is to explain why, on November 23, 1968, I was sitting in the student section on the *Harvard* side of Harvard Stadium when the astounding events of that afternoon began to unfold. Choosing Harvard had been a no-brainer for me. My family had no connection to the place. It had been a great pleasure to inform my father, whom I loved, that I would be attending Harvard. He pretended that he hadn't heard me correctly and said, "*Hart*ford? Did you say *Hart*ford University?"

At Harvard my pre-existing enthusiasm for still photography evolved into a passion for making movies. I majored in *Architectural Sciences* which was then really a fancy name for "Art Department" or "Design Department." I made student films for credit and actually graduated *cum laude*.

Since then I have been an independent documentary film producer. My movies have tended towards the "political" (*The Atomic Café, Feed, Blood in the Face, The Last Cigarette*, etc.). I've also contributed camera work for other directors (Michael Moore, *Roger and Me*; Chris Hegedus and D.A. Pennebaker, *The War Room*).

In the latter part of 2006 I was casting about for a new idea for a film. I can't pinpoint exactly the moment when the idea for *Harvard Beats Yale 29-29* came into my head. It probably had something to do with the fact that my only child, my daughter Madeleine, had just been accepted to Yale. Memories of my own college days were coming back to me. In any case, suddenly, there it was . . . *an idea*.

I obtained a videotape of the telecast of the game, stuck it in the machine, sat down and relived that unbelievable day. Absolutely incredible. It was, if possible, even more dramatic than I remembered. My idea for the movie was simple: *let the players tell the story*.

The first step was to secure permission to use portions of the game film; which I did.

Next I had to find the players. Using an assortment of alumni resources, reunion books, etc., I collected current addresses for a total of sixty-four of the players from both the Yale and Harvard teams.

I wrote them a letter outlining the project and asking if they would agree to be interviewed. I said that I would come to them . . . at their home, office, local pub— wherever they liked . . . and we would sit down with a small Hi-Def camera and talk for forty minutes or so. I emphasized that *they and only they* would tell the story; that there would be no added narration. (I've never used narration in a film.)

After follow-up phone calls sixty-one of the players said yes. [The one big disappointment in this project was that Calvin Hill, Yale's legendary halfback—who would be a first round draft pick with the Dallas Cowboys, Rookie of the Year and eventually an inductee into the NFL Hall of Fame—declined. He said, "I've talked enough about this game."]

Having lived in Manhattan since 1982, I didn't own a car. Four thousand dollars got me a slightly dinged-up 1996 Audi A4 Quattro with 140,000 miles on the odometer. (This odometer would soon read 155,000 miles.) My wife Paula bought me a GPS navigator.

I put a rack on the back of the car for my electric-assisted 5-speed bike (I'm a bit gimpy, walking . . . an ankle, a knee, etc.) and I was ready.

And then, in the spring of 2007, began an extraordinary journey. The players, especially the Yale players, lived all over the country. One of the Yalies lived in China. For some reason—I can only speculate—a disproportionate number of the Harvard players lived within an hour or two of Harvard Stadium.

I began with day trips into New Jersey and Connecticut. Harvard safety Pat Conway provided the most vivid of these early interviews. His story—beginning as a Harvard running back, dropping out of school, joining the Marines, being sent to Vietnam, fighting in the Siege of Khe Sanh, returning to Harvard to play defense, his reaction to the political turmoil on campus—later became the framework for a sequence in the film about how the Harvard players related to the chaos and upheavals of 1968.

Next I moved my base of operations from New York to a bed-and-breakfast in Cambridge near Harvard Square. Over the course of several weeks I interviewed nineteen players in Massachusetts, New Hampshire and Maine.

Before beginning shooting the film I had been a bit apprehensive about how I would be received by some of these ex-football players. I'm a slightly scruffy, borderline bohemian, independent (read: often unemployed) filmmaker. Some of these guys are now captains of industry and finance. Many are not . . . but certainly there are quite a few millionaires and a possible billionaire or two. My concerns proved totally groundless. These guys welcomed me warmly and shared their stories with enthusiasm. I think it was because we had something in common despite our differences: a moment in time forty years ago . . . a time and a place . . . not just the football but also the still-vivid memory of what it was like to be in these schools in that extraordinary year 1968.

I made new friends as I went along: effervescent Yale safety J. P. Goldsmith and his wife Hope; Harvard linebacker Neil Hurley and wife Kathy, who would later join my family for a weekend at the beach.

The interview with Harvard back-up quarterback Frank Champi would be crucial to the success of the project. Champi, a junior with little varsity experience at the time of the game, had taken over the Harvard offense late in the second quarter with the score Yale 22, Harvard 0. His subsequent performance has become the stuff of legend. In the years following the game he had . . . famously . . . shunned publicity. When I first contacted him he was ambivalent, to say the least, about doing the interview. I told him this was not going to be *The Frank Champi Story*, and, finally, he agreed to do it.

At 1:00pm Sunday, May 6, 2007 I pulled up in front of Frank Champi's house in Newburyport, Massachusetts. He greeted me on the sidewalk and helped me carry my gear into his house, which I took to be a good sign. In his kitchen I began to set up my tripod and he said, essentially . . . *wait a minute. . . .*

Then: *he* interviewed *me*. We sat, in his kitchen, for half an hour, and, for lack of a better expression, *he checked me out*.

Then, he said, "OK."

Then, I put the camera on the tripod, set up the light and attached the little Tram microphones to him and me.

Then, I put my head-phones on.

Then, all I could hear was his refrigerator.

Then I said, "Frank, we need to lose the refrigerator."

Then he said something like . . . *well, that will be a problem*. But he added that his refrigerator was on a thermostat, and, soon, it would turn itself off.

Then we sat . . . for some time . . . and the refrigerator did not go silent.

Then, I said, "Look man, let's unplug it."

Then he said, "No." (It would require pulling the thing way out of its place to do that.)

Then I said, "Most refrigerators have a control dial. Right inside of the door."

Then, reluctantly, he opened the door, saw the dial and turned it off.

The interview that ensued was extraordinary for many reasons, not the least of which was that the self-described "introspective," indeed notoriously *shy*, Champi *opened up* to me in ways, and on subjects, that I could never have anticipated. It was wonderful and I'm grateful to him for it. Most of my interviews run for about forty minutes. His went for ninety minutes and would have gone longer if I hadn't had another one scheduled for that evening a hundred miles away. At the end, Frank, who is, among other things, an inventor, demonstrated for me one of his inventions. It is a new kind of snow shovel. Elegantly simple in design, it eliminates using your back muscles from the process of shoveling snow. It works.

One other day stands out in my memory of the New England interviews. Three of the players opted to come to me, rather than having me come to their home or office. This meant them coming to my little bed-and-breakfast hotel room near Harvard Square. By some weird coincidence these three scheduled their interviews on the *same day*. They were: Harvard captain Vic Gatto; Yale captain Brian Dowling; Yale defensive captain Mike Bouscaren.

It was a Tuesday. Gatto arrived first, at 8:00am. He was remarkably unchanged from the smiling, dynamic figure I remembered walking about the campus forty years earlier. At some point during the interview I told him that Dowling would be arriving at 10:00 am and asked if he would be willing to wait so that I could film the two captains together for a few minutes. Although it would mean being late for a meeting, Vic graciously agreed.

Dowling called to say he was stuck in traffic and would be a bit late. He called again to say he was passing Harvard Stadium and would arrive in a few minutes. Vic Gatto and I greeted him in the driveway to the hotel. The two old friends shook hands. We went in to my room.

I was quite excited. I hadn't planned it this way but here were the two legendary captains together in front of my camera. I turned the camera "on" (or at least I thought I did), hoping to capture a bit of spontaneous chit-chat while I was attaching their microphones. Perhaps I was a bit *over*-excited. Then I "filmed" about ten minutes of their reminiscences as they sat side by side. Then Gatto left for his meeting and I interviewed Brian Dowling alone.

After Dowling left I was feeling quite pleased with myself. I replayed the Gatto interview. Good interview, good sound, good picture. Good. Next would be Gatto and Dowling together. *But what's this*? I'm looking at Dowling alone. His interview. What happened to the ten minutes of Gatto and Dowling together?

The lesson here for aspiring filmmakers is that it is important, indeed *necessary,* actually, to turn the camera *on* when filming something.

I was devastated, but I didn't have time to wallow in self-pity because I had a third interview to do that day.

Yale linebacker and defensive captain Mike Bouscaren arrived promptly at 4:00pm that afternoon. Tall, trim, well-dressed in a suit, he said he was " . . . involved in the investment world." To this day, he runs in "ultra marathons" (100 kilometer races) and has written two books on the subject.

In the interview he was calm, thoughtful, measured . . . and astonishingly candid. In the subsequent movie he has a compelling screen presence and emerges as perhaps the most memorable character. While describing his role in the game, he "confesses" that he felt that he had to be *the bad guy*. It's true that he was responsible for two key penalties against Yale in the final moments of the game that may have resulted from his over-enthusiasm. (I hadn't realized this, because you can't identify the culprit from the game film.)

Early audiences of the film [I'm writing this two weeks after the film premiered at the Toronto Film Festival] seemed to relate to Bouscaren as the villain of the piece or, indeed, *the man you love to hate*, which, to me, is unjust, or, at least, unfortunate. Each time he "confessed" to one of his "crimes" he did so with complete honesty and took responsibility himself. He never blamed a ref. He said the penalties against him were correct and fair (in one case ending forty years of controversy). "I got what I deserved," he said.

At the end of the film I give Mike Bouscaren the second-to-last word. He talks about what the game has meant to him in his life and how it taught him, among other things, humility.

I returned to New York to regroup and prepare for a month-long counter-clockwise zig-zag circumnavigation of the United States by car. Cleveland, Chicago, Minneapolis, Vail, Reno, San Francisco, Bakersfield, Las Vegas, Los Angeles, San Diego, San Antonio, Arkansas, North Carolina and many points in between.

I set out in the second week of June, 2007.

It had been thirty years since I had driven across the country. In the early 1970's I used to do it almost capriciously . . . in pursuit of this or that film project or this or that girlfriend. In 1975 I drove with my brother Pierce from San Francisco to Boston in fifty-four hours (in a Volkswagon bus!), never stopping, in order to get to a World Series game in Fenway Park.

Now, in the course of this present journey, two things struck me that had changed in the American landscape.

First: the windmills. This was new and, to me, wonderful. They appeared with increasing frequency as I headed west. By the time I was in California I expected to see them daily. In west Texas I passed a seemingly endless string of them—mile after mile—giant blades turning slowly . . . awe inspiring . . . magnificent.

Second: the malls, or, perhaps I should say, the *franchises*. Small town America is still small town America; but there is a Wal-Mart. It is not my intention here to wax nostalgic about the good old days. In fact, I want to *celebrate* one of these franchises: Applebee's.

Imagine this: You've been driving for ten or twelve hours. It is 9:00pm. You are in a strange town. You want a steak and a glass of Bushmills Irish whisky. You want to know how the Mets did today. You push the "restaurant" button on your GPS navigator and then select "Applebee's." Twelve minutes later you are sitting at your favorite seat, at the curved end of the long, horseshoe-shaped bar with your whiskey in front of you, three sports channels playing silently on the TVs above your head . . . and your steak is cooking (medium rare).

In town after town, state after state, I repeated this scenario. The Applebee's were identical but the people were not.

In Bakersfield I sat next to a young woman who was talking on her cell phone to her father for the first time in five years. She was going to get married again. She wanted him to come to the wedding. "This time it's going to be different, Daddy." She was crying.

In Emporia, Virginia, on a Friday night, I took my usual seat at the end of the horseshoe. To my right was a somewhat rowdy group of black teenagers . . . three guys and a girl . . . dressed hip-hop grunge . . . drinking pitchers of beer . . . enjoying themselves. A white truck driver sat down to my left. A moment later he leaned towards me, nodded towards the teenagers and said, "Those *Democrats* are making too much noise." This may have been true but my response ("*I'm* a Democrat") shocked him into silence. Further to my left a well-dressed, elderly white couple was finishing their dinner. The woman got up, approached the teenagers, and gave one of the guys a big hug. It seems they all knew one another. From Applebee's! Later, the teenagers, having decided that they didn't want to drink the final pitcher of beer that they had ordered, asked me to ask "my friend" (the truck driver) whether he would like it. Flummoxed, he declined, but very politely.

I stayed in cheap motels along the way. In the mornings I would fill my thermos with black coffee from the pot in the lobby and proceed. I didn't use maps. Sometimes I wasn't sure what state I was in but it didn't matter. The GPS navigator led me efficiently from interview to motel to interview. Once, and only once, it failed me. It led me down a dirt road in the middle of a corn field at night and told me that I had arrived at my motel. A machine with a sense of humor?

Several players, from both Yale and Harvard, put me up for the night. In Incline Village, Nevada (a mountainside community overlooking Lake Tahoe) I arrived at the home of Yale defensive tackle (and future captain) Tom Neville for a 5:00 pm interview. His wife Kelly greeted me at the door and asked whether I wanted to go to a wine-tasting dinner before doing the interview. I didn't know what to say. Neville joined us and it was agreed that we would go. We drove down to the lake and then boarded a privately hired bus which took us along the lake to a magnificent old stone lodge where the dinner would be held. There were many courses to be served. There were many wines to be tasted. Neville doesn't drink. I do. The dinner went on for hours. Everyone was having a fine time—but there was a bizarre, almost Edgar

Allen Poe-like, sub-text to this story. This was the weekend that a large portion of the wooded hillside surrounding Lake Tahoe burnt to the ground. Some of the guests at the dinner had been evacuated from their houses. Many homes were being destroyed as we ate and drank. We could see the smoke across the lake. When, finally, we had returned to Neville's home it was midnight. We did the interview, despite the late hour. Neville was sharp and engaging but your cameraman/interviewer may not have been on top of his game. Then he gave me a bed, for which I thank him.

In the interviews there were many wonderful stories that I simply couldn't fit into the narrative of the project.

Yale tackle Rich Mattas, a nuclear physicist, described his life-long quest for the holy grail of energy supply: *fusion*.

Harvard middle guard Alex MacLean showed me some of his stunningly beautiful aerial photographs. An internationally renowned photographer, MacLean works alone, flying the plane and taking the pictures himself.

I asked Harvard tight end Pete Varney whether catching the pass in the end zone for two points on the final play of the game was the highlight of his athletic career. He had to think about it. He was a little embarrassed. Then, modestly, he described hitting his first home run in the major leagues . . . *against the Yankees*. (Varney had gone on to play catcher for the White Sox. He is now the baseball coach at Brandeis.)

Yale guard Jack Perkowski gave me a brief description of what it is like being the largest manufacturer of automotive parts in The People's Republic of China. (For more on this, read his book *Managing the Dragon: How I'm Building a Billion-Dollar Business in China*, from Crown Publishing).

Harvard safety Pat Conway told me how he negotiated himself out of a contract to play for the then-worst team in the NFL: the Pittsburgh Steelers (who would be hiring a rookie quarterback the following year named Terry Bradshaw).

Yale defensive guard Mick Kleber described an extraordinary career trajectory. After Yale he was: a Marine platoon commander in Vietnam, a Navy social aide in the Nixon White House, a Marine Corps representative to the Bicentennial Committee, a rock video pioneer in Hollywood in the 1980s (he produced over 700 of them for top bands), etc., etc. and he is currently writing a screenplay for the Weinstein brothers.

My interview with Harvard defensive end (and future captain) John Cramer took place in a motel room in Williamsburg, Virginia. Cramer was dripping with sweat. He had just (and I do mean *at just that moment*) completed a twenty-three day bicycle trip across the country.

Yale cornerback John Waldman, who was in the game for *one* play (which proved to be pivotal) and who is now a celebrated pediatric neurosurgeon, described how the discipline he developed playing on the football team helped get him through medical school.

The interview with Harvard guard Tommy Lee Jones began badly. Both of us being in the movie business (!), we had conflicting ideas about how to attach the little microphone to his body. (I wanted to run the wire up under his shirt. He said it wasn't necessary.) I won that battle but the war was just beginning. I would ask him a question, he would stare at me for a while . . . and then say something. Sometimes what he said related to my question. Sometimes it did not. I didn't really care because almost everything he said was interesting to me on some level. But there was tension. *The New Yorker* recently described Jones as America's foremost dead-pan comedian. I believe I know what they meant. His contemplative, death-stare silences became an integral part of the interview. After about thirty-five minutes of this I told him I was done and asked whether there was anything that he wished I had asked him but hadn't. He said *no* but that *he liked hearing stories about the game and did I know any more*? (I had told him a few stories about his teammates.) I said yes I do and proceeded to tell him the following story:

My father played football for Yale. He was at the game, sitting on the Yale side. I, of course, was sitting on the Harvard side. After the game I found him in the crowd and said, "Dad, how did you like the game?" You have to understand that my father had been in the Marines in WW2 and had lost many friends when he landed at Guam and Iwo Jima. He also lost his older brother, my uncle Kevin, to the Nazis. So I said, "Dad, how did you like the game?" He looked me in the eye and said, "Worst day of my life."

And now, for the first time, Mr. Tommy Lee Jones laughed. We found other things to talk about and the interview continued . . . with less tension.

But it was in Wilmington, North Carolina, at the home of Yale middle guard Dick Williams, that the strangest, and most wonderful, event of my journey began to unfold.

Before interviewing Williams I had met his (very beautiful) wife Maria and his two (very beautiful) teenage daughters. One of his daughters, Daniela, has ideas of becoming a filmmaker. She wanted to stay in the room and watch me shoot the interview. This put me in a quandary. I wanted to be alone with Williams . . . so I suggested a compromise: She would leave us alone and, later, I would send her a video of the entire interview. She agreed, I did the interview and went on my way.

When I had returned to New York I wrote an encouraging note to Daniela and sent her a copy of the interview. I also sent a copy of the game film. Some time later I received a letter from Dick Williams which ended with these words:

I need to make you aware of an incident that took place here that directly relates to your decision to make my interview tape available. My wife, Maria, and I happened to be going through a rough patch recently based on differences over child-rearing philosophy and personal finances. Several days ago, she had actually moved out of the master bedroom into the guest bedroom and began sleeping alone. We were barely speaking to one another (and I am certain both of us were fantasizing about an eventual marital break-up), when I received a telephone call at work yesterday in which she exclaimed in a bright, cheerful voice, "I have been watching your interview on that videotape . . . you were GREAT!" With that, the tide turned completely and she announced that she was moving back into our bedroom. Later that evening, over a glass of red wine at our neighborhood Italian eatery, she looked into my eyes and said, "You know, watching your interview and seeing you in that football game made me fall in love with you all over again." Given that I felt like an exile in Siberia only hours before that, I was overcome with emotion. [He then adds a few kind words about me and signs off:] *Best regards, Dick Williams.*

Back in New York, interviews completed, I hunkered down in my Greenwich Village basement office to cut the film. In the past I have been known to labor obsessively, perhaps *over*-obsessively, on this stage of the filmmaking process. Not so this time. The movie seemed to cut itself. It was a real *joy* putting it together. I couldn't wait to get up in the morning and get back at it.

At some point during this process I was sitting on a bar stool in my local pub, a few blocks from my office, filibustering about the movie when a nearby stranger piped up and said, "I want that book." A few drinks and a handshake later I had a publisher for a book version of my movie. Aaron Schlechter, a young editor at The Overlook Press, likes to do business the Texas way. (That's where he's from.)

As the editing of the film progressed I was, as usual, becoming "attached" to some of the key characters. They may have spent only an hour or two with me but now I was spending days, weeks, indeed months with them. Their voices, inflections, mannerisms and personalities were becoming as familiar to me as the "real" people in my life.

Thus it was with shock, and deep sadness, that I learned of the death of Harvard tackle Fritz Reed, one of the unlikely heroes of the game. I had interviewed Fritz in tandem with his friend Harvard fullback Gus Crim. The two of them together provided an exuberant and amusing counterpoint as they recalled the events of that day. Now, upon hearing of Fritz' death, it was almost like losing an old friend.

I finished the movie early in the spring of 2008 and began sending it around to see if anybody was going to be interested in it. This was an anxious time. I had financed it myself and was now in debt. The movie business, especially today, especially for independent films, can be brutal. Too many films. Too few screens. And those screens filled with "safe" Hollywood product.

I had sent the movie to Karen Cooper who runs *Film Forum*, a legendary "art house" in New York City and perhaps America's premier launching pad for truly independent movies. I had previously opened four movies there, going back to 1982, but I wasn't too optimistic this time. Karen didn't strike me as much of a football fan, to say the least. A few weeks later the phone in my office rang and a woman's voice said, "Kevin, I love this movie."

I said, "That's great. Who's calling?"

The voice said, "It's Karen and I love this movie. No I don't *love* this movie. I *lurve* this movie." (She had just been showing *Annie Hall* in which Woody Allen expresses his feelings for Diane Keaton similarly, a reference that I didn't get at the time.)

This was most excellent.

Karen later confessed that she had seen exactly one half of one football game in her life, back in the 60s, and had left in disgust when some of the Dartmouth fans began tormenting the Princeton mascot.

More good news would follow: an invitation to the Toronto Film Festival, a great *Variety* review, other openings arranged, a distribution deal. At this writing (in September of 2008) it is too soon to predict the ultimate fate of the movie but it looks as if it will at least have a chance to find its audience.

My previous movies have tended to be about things of which I . . . how shall I say this? . . . *disapproved* . . . (white supremacists, U.S. Government atom bomb propaganda in the '50s, the tobacco industry, etc.).

Harvard Beats Yale 29-29 is something new for me: a celebration of something wonderful.

Traveling the country, finding these ex-football players, sharing their memories . . . I had more *fun* making this movie than I've had since I began making student films forty-two years ago. Being with these guys was definitely more pleasant than, for instance, hanging out with the Ku Klux Klan. They were great. So, to the football players, *thank you*.

This is their story.

—KEVIN RAFFERTY
New York City
September 26, 2008

YALE

Yale tackle,
George Bass

Yale linebacker and
defensive captain,
Mike Bouscaren

Yale linebacker and
future captain (1969),
Andy Coe

Yale halfback,
Nick Davidson

Yale captain and quarterback, **Brian Dowling**

Yale defensive tackle, **Fran Gallagher** (on the left)

Yale defensive end, **Jim Gallagher** (on the right)

Yale tackle, **Kyle Gee**

Yale safety,
J.P. Goldsmith

Yale monster back,
Ron Kell

Yale defensive tackle,
Mick Kleber

Yale guard,
Brad Lee

Yale fullback,
Bob Levin

Yale tackle,
Ted Livingston

Yale defensive end,
Pat Madden

Yale end,
Del Marting

Yale defensive tackle,
Rich Mattas

Yale center,
Fred Morris

Yale defensive tackle
and future captain (1970),
Tom Neville

Yale tackle,
Tom Peacock

Yale guard,
Jack Perkowski

Yale middle guard,
Milt Puryear

Yale defensive end,
Scott Robinson

Yale cornerback,
John Waldman

Yale end,
Bruce Weinstein

Yale middle guard,
Dick Williams

HARVARD

Harvard cornerback,
Mike Ananis

Harvard halfback,
John Ballantyne

Harvard defensive tackle,
Rick Berne

Harvard back-up quarterback,
Frank Champi

Harvard safety,
Pat Conway

Harvard defensive end
and future captain (1969),
John Cramer

Harvard fullback,
Gus Crim
(on the right)

Harvard tackle,
Bob Dowd

Harvard linebacker
and defensive captain,
John Emery

Harvard linebacker
and future captain (1970),
Gary Farneti

Harvard end,
Bruce Freeman

Harvard cornerback,
Rick Frisbie

Harvard captain and halfback,
Vic Gatto

Harvard defensive end,
Pete Hall

Harvard halfback,
Ray Hornblower

Harvard cornerback,
Neil Hurley

Harvard cornerback,
John Ignacio

Harvard guard,
Bob Jannino

Harvard guard,
Tommy Lee Jones

Harvard defensive tackle,
Lonny Kaplan

Harvard defensive back,
Bill Kelly

Harvard end,
John Kiernan

Harvard quarterback,
George Lalich

Harvard middle guard,
Alex MacLean

Harvard linebacker,
Jerry Marino

Harvard defensive end,
Joe McKinney

Harvard linebacker,
Dale Neal

Harvard defensive end,
Steve Ranere

Harvard tackle,
Fritz Reed

Harvard halfback,
Jim Reynolds

Harvard punter,
Gary Singleterry

Harvard center,
Ted Skowronski

Harvard defensive back (and onside kicking specialist), **Ken Thomas**

Harvard end, **Pete Varney**

Harvard safety, **Tom Wynne**

PROLOGUE

Yale tackle, Tom Peacock: You just got the feeling that the universe had shifted somehow and that something portentous . . . significant . . . weird . . . was taking place.

Harvard center, Ted Skowronski: You had the sense it wasn't real . . . it was happening . . . but . . . yet. . . .

Yale middle guard, Dick Williams: . . . almost like an out-of-body experience where you're watching things happen and you can't believe that it's happening.

Yale safety, J.P. Goldsmith: It wasn't painful. It was too strange to be painful.

Yale end, Bruce Weinstein: I think it was just a slow motion nightmare.

Harvard guard, Tommy Lee Jones: I remember telling myself to be cool and stay smooth and *think*. . . .

part one

BEFORE THE GAME

1

ARRIVING AT YALE

Yale guard, Jack Perkowski: You know, before I went to Yale, Carm [Yale coach Carmen Cozza] sent all the incoming freshmen a copy of the book by Tim Cohane called *The Yale Football Story*, which I religiously read before I arrived at the Yale campus my freshman year. And of course that tells the whole tradition of Yale football, and Yale was a tremendous football powerhouse. In fact, a lot of the modern game of football was really started at Yale. So, I knew that I was joining a long football tradition.

Yale tackle, Tom Peacock: I grew up in the Midwest, and I grew up in a house, actually, where I was never quite sure. . . . I mean, I knew the priorities were education, Presbyterianism, and football. . . .

Yale tackle, Kyle Gee: I came from a very tiny community in southern Virginia, which is near nothing. The nearest town that had a movie you could go to was about thirty-five miles away. So, when I showed up at Yale, I was really a fish out of water. I was lucky to be there for early football practice and to meet a lot of guys from all over the country, so that when the school year started, I already had this set of people that I knew and a set of friendships that was starting.

Yale middle guard, Milton Puryear: Before I got there, I'd been a member of the Student Non-violent Coordinating Committee [SNCC] in Washington, D.C. . . . helped organize and taught at a liberation school and I'd been to the March on Washington with my family . . . so I was very much attuned to those issues. . . . I wasn't a square by any means.

Yale center, Fred Morris: I grew up in a town of about seventeen or eighteen thousand in Indiana. My mom had been trained as a nurse. My dad was a Chevy dealer in this small town, Newcastle, Indiana. I'd never been east of Columbus until I was a junior in high school. I certainly wasn't prepared for the whole east coast thing, because I'd never *been* to the east coast. I think I was pretty reserved. I mean, I came into Yale—I'd promised my dad, he asked me and I promised him, that I wouldn't drink until I was twenty-one, so that set me apart right away. I'd never written a paper more than five pages long before I went to Yale. It was a pretty intimidating place to be for a year, year and a half. And then, after that, I did well, and I thought, *well you know, hell, I belong here.*

Yale end, Bruce Weinstein: Midterm freshman year, my college dean told me that I should probably quit football and concentrate on my studies. I was having a lot of trouble and I was close to tears at the time. I was captain of the freshman team and I couldn't see quitting. I made some Herculean effort, as far as I was concerned, and wound up getting through the first semester OK.

Yale safety, J.P. Goldsmith: It was one of the worst times of my life. Everything everybody ever did around me at Yale, they were better than I was. They were smarter. They were better football players. They got dates and I didn't. I was pretty miserable, to the point where I talked to my father . . . *maybe this isn't for me.* I was going to join the army. And my father said, "That's great. Have a nice experience in the army, and I hope you can find some way to help pay for your education when you get out." So that was the end of that. But it was a struggle.

I went to public high school in central Pennsylvania and I was a star. I was used to getting my name in the *Harrisburg Patriot News.* I was used to having my papers get A's. I remember writing my first English paper [at Yale] . . . English 15, freshman English . . . on "Bartleby the Scrivener." This is a short story by Herman Melville and I thought I had written the most magnifi- cent expository piece of writing in the history of humankind. I got a 70. OK? Sixty-nine doesn't even pass. I was humbled, to say the least. And then, I was one of seventeen quar- terbacks on the freshman team and I was the third-string quarterback and the second- string safety. And that's the way it was. It was pretty humbling.

"I was the third-string quarterback . . ."

KR: *So, when did it get better?*

It was a struggle to get better. It didn't get better, really, until I was a sophomore. I have Coach Carmen Cozza to thank for that. And no matter what kind of coach he is or isn't—and he's a Hall of Fame coach—this is a world-class human being. He sat me down and said, "You can play a lot of football here. Do you want to play quarterback or do you want to play football?" So, that was an easy decision, and I went from third-string quarterback, second-string safety on the freshman team to starting [at safety] the very first game my sophomore year. By dint of pure luck . . . one kid flunked out (yes, occasionally somebody does) and somebody else decided he was just going to play hockey. So, there I was.

I am of the Jewish persuasion, and the first game was Yom Kippur, holiest day of the Jewish calendar. My father is a very observant Hebrew, and a good guy, and a great football fan. And Hank Greenberg or Sandy Koufax wouldn't be particularly proud of me. He said, "You play, I'll pray." And that's how it started.

Yale middle guard, Dick Williams: Well, it was almost magical. . . . Our freshman team was undefeated. So, there were glimpses of all that greatness, even then, I mean in the very beginning. You could see . . . especially Brian Dowling, the quarterback. He was profes- sional, even then. He seemed much older than his years, even as a freshman, and he had a sort of cool *nonchalance* which he employed. It made us all believe.

Yale linebacker, Mike Bouscaren: I guess I could start when Calvin [Yale halfback Calvin Hill] scored six touchdowns against Princeton our freshman year. We knew that Brian and Calvin were terrific athletes, and I think Calvin showed out first.

Yale tackle, George Bass: There were high expectations, because some of these people were highly recruited. I didn't realize until I got there. I wasn't recruited. I was a walk-on. But I was told that there were headlines in the Cleveland paper when Brian Dowling decided to go to Yale, of all places. And so, there were some high profile athletes that ended up on that team.

> *KR (asks Brian Dowling): You were one of the most heavily recruited high school football players in the country. I think I read somewhere that when Woody Hayes figured out that he wasn't going to get you at Ohio State, he urged you to go Yale so that you wouldn't be playing against Ohio State.*

Yale captain and quarterback, Brian Dowling: Well, one of the schools that was in my last four, final four, was Michigan, and Woody Hayes didn't want to be playing against me. In fact, he called Carm [Yale coach Carmen Cozza], whom he had coached at Miami of Ohio, and he said, "I don't want him to go to Michigan, so if he's not going to come here, really put the full court press on him." So . . . Carm told me that story. It's pretty funny.

2

ARRIVING AT HARVARD

Harvard quarterback, George Lalich: The thought of going to Harvard or anyplace out east was just foreign to me. You have to understand the concept of *Harvard* to somebody from South Chicago around the steel mills. It was something just out of the realm of your thoughts. I remember when the acceptance came from Harvard. I was in bed and my dad came in and said, "I've got great news for you. You're going to Harvard. You've been accepted to Harvard." And I think my first thought was, "Oh my God, what am I going to do?"

Harvard end, Bruce Freeman: I was a public high school kid. My family didn't have any money, so I wasn't able to visit. In fact, I don't think I'd been east of the Mississippi. So I just came up into Harvard Square with my suitcases and walked across the street and tried to find somebody to get me into a dorm.

Harvard cornerback, Neil Hurley: Catholic high school. Eight years before that of Catholic grammar school with nuns. Most of my classmates' parents had brogues or Italian accents. To go over to Harvard Square and Harvard University was a little bit of a culture shock. I met all sorts of different people. To me, a minority was somebody who wasn't Irish Catholic.

Harvard defensive end, Joe McKinney: I lived in Holworthy as a freshman. One of the first people I met was a guy named Josh Waletzky. Josh was from New York, and the typical deal: *How are you? Who are you? What did you do this summer?* Well, I was at home working construction to make money to come to school. "What did you do, Josh?"

Joe McKinney

Josh Waletzky

"I taught a course at Columbia this summer."
I said, "You're an entering freshman, right?"
"Yeah."
"What did you teach a course in?"
"I taught a course in linguistics."
Well I didn't know what linguistics was. And he said, "I've written a book, you know, and it's published. . . ."
And I'm thinking *OK McKinney, I'm from Clear Creek High School [Texas] where I was a pretty good student. I did all the things. I was president of the class. I was All-District in three sports. I had scholarships to go play ball. Do I even know enough to write, in a blue book,* you know, the proverbial blue book that you take exams in, *do I know enough to start writing, let alone write a whole book?* I mean, that was my introduction to Harvard.

Harvard cornerback, John Ignacio: My father was a farmer from Guam. My mother never graduated from high school in Boston and always said to me, "I just hope you graduate from high school." I was the first person of Guamanian descent ever to go to Harvard.

Harvard center, Ted Skowronski: My father and mother were both factory workers. They graduated eighth grade education. That was as high as they went.

Harvard back-up quarterback, Frank Champi: I came from a working class environment, a public high school. I did well in high school and was a decent student, but I wasn't prepared for the Ivy League experience, especially the Harvard experience. It was very intimidating at first. Made for a lot of anxious moments. I had a very difficult time adjusting, especially to the academic part of the experience.

Harvard quarterback, George Lalich: A lot of the guys on the football team were working class, Boston-area guys, just by happenstance, who were roommates or good friends of mine. But also the guys that went to Andover and Exeter were really down to earth and good guys. So, my first experiences there were with the *people*—and that's what really made the place so good. It wasn't so much the academics. It was the quality and the decency of the people that I met, became friends with and played with.

Harvard halfback, Ray Hornblower: I came from a privileged background. My grandfather and father grew up on Beacon Hill, and my grandmother was from St. Louis. . . . They definitely partook of the better things in American life. But at the same time, it was. . . . We were pretty serious about sports...and sports is a great leveler . . . so I found Harvard a welcome environment in that regard.

Harvard quarterback, George Lalich: I remember coming out for the first freshman football practice, and they'd say, you know, "All the ends, line up here." And a few guys would line up. "And all the tackles line up here and the defensive backs line up here. OK, all the *quarterbacks* line up here." And there were like twenty of us. And every one of us was All-State from Arkansas or Ohio or California or Michigan and had turned down scholarships to Notre Dame and Michigan State. The competition was kind of tough . . . and eventually it got to be a war of attrition.

3

SUPERHEROES

Yale captain and quarterback, Brian Dowling:
There was an article about me in *Sports Illustrated* about fifteen, seventeen years ago. It was quite a long article. I was working in New York at the time, and one of the guys, a salesman next to me, said, after he read the article, "What would have happened if they had let Calvin [Yale halfback Calvin Hill] play quarterback?" Because he was a quarterback in high school. And he was 51-0 in high school. He ran twenty-five times a game and threw twenty-five times a game. And I said that I would have played another position. I was good enough not to sit on the bench. I've asked Carm [Yale coach Carmen Cozza] this too. I said, "What made the decision for you to switch him and not me?" And he said, "I think you just had that something extra that that's the decision we made." Plus, I don't know if the '60s were ready for a black quarterback at a white school. There weren't any black quarterbacks playing major college football in the '60s, unless at Grambling or Jackson State. So, I don't know if that had anything to do with it, but that was sort of . . . that might have been sort of the underlying mentality . . . that we didn't have black quarterbacks. I don't think major colleges had them until, probably, at least the mid-'70s.

Yale captain and quarterback Brian Dowling

Yale halfback Calvin Hill

Yale tackle, Kyle Gee: Brian and Calvin were two guys who really kept their own counsel. I didn't know either one of them, personally, all that well. Calvin was a very, very religious guy and a quiet guy.

Yale halfback Calvin Hill

Yale captain and quarterback, Brian Dowling: Calvin is a shy person, for the most part. Soft spoken. We roomed together on away trips, which weren't many; we'd only play three away games each year. So, I got to know him a little bit more. But he was just very quiet....

Yale end, Bruce Weinstein: Calvin was a sincere person, an interesting student. Practice was not his favorite chore, and it was a chore. He would practice . . . mostly. Sometimes we'd be getting on the bus to go to practice and, having talked to Calvin at the bus stop, once we got going we'd realize he wasn't with us. But he was generous; he was friendly; he was an easy-going guy; he had some real interest in some of his studies; and I found him to be a good friend.

Yale guard, Brad Lee: Well, they were campus idols in a way that probably couldn't happen any more. Both of them, really. They were, sort of... just stood out among all other students as a cut above the rest of us.

Yale middle guard, Milton Puryear: Well, the two of them were larger than life. Brian Dowling, people called him *God*. That's what his nickname was among the fans, because he managed to turn a really bad situation into a gain so often.

Yale captain and quarterback, Brian Dowling: I was pretty much anonymous walking around campus, because I was just another 6'2" white kid.

> *KR: Now wait a second, Brian. I have to interrupt you here. Did you not have a nickname on campus? A three-letter nick-name that begins with G?*

Well, that was . . . well . . . you're somewhat anonymous because you play football and you wear a helmet. In my uniform I was recognizable but not walking around campus. People are in the stands; they can't see your face. Calvin, on the other hand, being 6'4", being 230, being black…everybody knew who he was from the moment he stepped on campus.

Yale linebacker, Mike Bouscaren: Calvin and Brian continued to do just extraordinary things on the field. Things that were unimaginable. Things that were beyond the scope of ordinary Ivy League football players. The things that they would do and come up with, the imagination, the improvisation, the third and longs that were converted into first-downs and then touchdowns just seemed to run in strings. And we came to depend on their ability to make things happen.

4

GOD PLAYS QUARTERBACK FOR YALE

Yale tackle, Rich Mattas: One of my roommates was so impressed with Dowling's athletic ability, that he was convinced that he was basically The Messiah . . . and that at the end of his college career in football, the clouds would part and a light would shine down and raise Brian to heaven at that point.

Yale tackle, Kyle Gee: Brian was. . . . When we played at Princeton, junior year, and won that game against Princeton for the first time in a long time, it was sleeting, and at the end of the game, the sun came out and the people in the stands started shouting, "Brian made the sun come out," or "Brian made the clouds go away."

Yale captain Brian Dowling

Yale cornerback, John Waldman: There was something special about Brian Dowling. He just had that . . . *aura* . . . that great athletes have. He just . . . he was a real leader, and he didn't have to say a word, he never dressed anybody down, he never was even cocky. He just. . . . He was just a winner. People just *believed* in Brian Dowling.

Yale halfback, Nick Davidson: There was a headline in the *Yale Daily News* saying "GOD PLAYS QUARTERBACK FOR YALE." So, you can imagine . . . different personalities would react differently. But I think Brian handled it with dignity and humility.

Yale end, Bruce Weinstein: Brian would hold court on Friday nights before home games from the little balcony off his room. . . .

Yale linebacker Andy Coe: . . . the crowds would go to the courtyard below Brian's room and look up and want God to come out and speak to them. You know, that kind of thing. That's how he was revered on the campus.

Yale defensive end, (and Brian Dowling's roommate) Scott Robinson: I think probably his most amazing quality was his humility, given the fact that he was so utterly successful during that time. I'm sure you've heard all the stories about how he was referred to as "God," with a capital "G," in the student newspaper. For the most part, the student body was pretty laid back in respect to athletics at Yale, but in my junior year at the end of the season, before the Princeton game, whom we hadn't beaten in six years, in the middle of the week, totally unrehearsed, hundreds of students gathered outside of our dorm room and were just chanting for him. They wanted him to come to the window and speak to them and make some statement about what he was going to do to Princeton that weekend. He was a big deal on that campus.

Yale safety, J.P. Goldsmith: Dowling had never lost a game. OK? In college, in high school . . . any game that he had ever finished he had never lost. [Actually, Dowling's undefeated record went back to the seventh grade.]

Yale tackle, Kyle Gee: He had this sort of ultimate calm that he seems always to have had. He never got excited. I mean. . . . He literally would draw up a play. You know, we're not supposed to be doing that. People would say to him *don't be making up plays in the huddle* but he would want to do it.

> **KR (asks J.P. Goldsmith):** *I heard that Dowling had a nickname?*

Yale safety, J.P. Goldsmith: God? You have to remember something. Yale was. . . . Women hadn't been invented yet, OK? Yale was still all male. You had to wear a coat and tie for all meals our first two years, and I assumed everybody liked to eat on a regular basis. Everybody had a coat and tie on, OK? It was a pretty boring place. You studied, you drank a little and you watched Brian Dowling and Calvin Hill play football . . . and the rest of us participated a little. He was a real thrill. It was something to do.

5

GLORY DAYS IN NEW HAVEN

Yale center, Fred Morris: I mean, that football team was. . . . It wasn't just a football team at Yale University. That football team. . . . This is going to sound like it's an overstatement, but it really kind of *inspired* that university and that campus. I mean [Yale University President] Kingman Brewster was a big fan of the football team.

Yale monster back, Ron Kell: I'll never forget Kingman Brewster leading a "Fuck Princeton" cheer from his doorstep. I thought that was amazing.

Yale University President
Kingman Brewster

Yale end, Bruce Weinstein: It was thrilling. The student body was incredibly supportive. We'd take off in busses for the away games in the '68 season, and probably the latter part of '67, and they'd be out there yelling, screaming, shaking the bus.

Yale fullback, Bob Levin: You could walk down the street and everyone would say hello to you and shopkeepers would put your picture up on their walls. So it was nothing I'd really anticipated when I thought about playing football in the Ivy League. The reaction was just overwhelming.

Yale guard, Jack Perkowski: Of course, every game we played was tremendous as far as attendance. I mean, they were filling up the Yale Bowl and the Yale Bowl is a big stadium with 60,000-plus seats.

Yale monster back Ron Kell: As a sophomore, and here I was at Yale, which you certainly don't associate with football, really, and looking up in the stands at the Yale Bowl, which is a pretty immense place, and seeing it. . . . There were a lot of people there. It was really an ocean of people in the stands at times and it was . . . it was a real high. It was pretty cool.

Yale cornerback, John Waldman: That season, the school really came together. I think the grade point average went up a couple of points because of the good feelings everyone had. Or that may have had to do with Margaret Mead who gave everyone in her class a grade of 100.

Yale defensive tackle, Mick Kleber: There were all these great pep rallies. It was like living the quintessential collegiate experience. For me, I would walk out of my rooms, across the campus in those days and literally feel like I was in a dream. I was just totally blown away by the whole thing and loving it. I was well aware that this was a terrific thing going on with us. The Blue Power phenomenon . . . and just the way everyone was energized by the whole thing.

Yale tackle, Kyle Gee: For us, it was very, very enjoyable. The down side was that we started to get, frankly, just a little too big for ourselves...and we didn't stay focused for the whole season. That was a big problem.

6

DOONESBURY, BUSH, GORE AND STREEP

Yale guard, Jack Perkowski: It really ignited the whole Yale campus. Everybody was into football. Before the games there were big rallies. Garry Trudeau started his *Doonesbury* comic strip, and the characters were "B.D." [Brian Dowling] and "The Tree" [Bruce Weinstein] and. . . . I can remember getting on the bus at the Payne Whitney gymnasium to go out to practice and everyone would be out there with a copy of the *Yale Daily News* to look and see what "B.D." had been up to that weekend.

Yale captain and quarterback, Brian Dowling ("B.D."): Well, Garry Trudeau started writing the strip under the name *Bull Tales* the fall of my senior year. He was a junior that year. And being one of the more visible people on campus, and the team being, you know, a very visible organization on campus, we were in the strip once or twice a week out of the five days. He had a very good sense of humor and the fact that we were winning sort of made the whole thing easier to take, if anybody had a thin skin, not that anybody on the football team did, that I was aware of. But it was interesting how we would go to the *Yale Daily* to find out if we were in the strip that day and what did we do. I think everyone really enjoyed it.

Yale defensive tackle, Tom Neville: To read the latest *Bull Tales* with Brian and Calvin and Bruce and all these guys starring in it . . . it was really spectacular.

Yale tackle, Rich Mattas: It took on a cult-like status because the members of the team, the offense in this case, were part of the comic strip. Everybody was reading the comic strip as time went on, including the football team of course, and every word was true.

Yale middle guard, Dick Williams: Oh well. . . . The comic strip to me was unbelievably insightful. I mean, I loved it.

Yale tackle, Kyle Gee: We were really taken with the comic strip. You know, we were really thrilled to be, although not always in it, to be part of it. And I was always distressed that my number was not used, but I got over it. It was a pretty big deal.

Yale end, Del Marting: He [cartoonist Garry Trudeau] was good because he did capture some of the, kind of, the interplay. He had some of the . . . some of the strips were about the huddle and . . . it was kind of entertaining. I mean, it wasn't cynical, it wasn't sarcastic, it was just a clever way of capturing some of the feeling and some of the tone of the times, at least with the football team. It was positive.

Yale tackle, George Bass: I was *in* one. He would use our numbers. 78 was my number, and I would be one of the anonymous linemen, but he did have one where Brian Dowling yells at me for letting a pass rusher in and making him have to do some famous moves to get out of it. In the comic strip, Garry Trudeau has me holding up my middle finger to his remark, and Dowling says, "Well, I have to respect that." So, that was my claim to fame, that I did make it into *Doonesbury* before it was a national treasure.

Yale end, Bruce Weinstein ("The Tree"): "The Tree" seemed to me uncharacteristic of me, of the individual me—some kind of philosophical person who would expound on one thing or another. And I was not in that often, but when I was, it seemed that I was somebody spouting off and lecturing. I don't know where it came from…and it didn't bear a lot of relation to who I was.

Yale defensive end, Pat Madden: The major people you could recognize in the strip were "B.D." for Brian, and Calvin, but also Del Marting was featured, and J.P. Goldsmith occasionally would show up.

Yale safety, J.P. Goldsmith: I think Mike "The Man" Doonesbury was actually Mike Bouscaren, who was the linebacker, number 27.

Bouscaren   *Doonesbury*

Yale linebacker, Mike Bouscaren: Well *Doonesbury* featured individuals on the football team in different settings. Sometimes, "B.D." would be in class with his football helmet on—funny perspectives of the football team. I think there was a certain amount of awe that Garry Trudeau had, but also I sensed that he had a certain amount of *fear* with regard to football players. And for those of us, myself... speaking for myself, I should say, the cartoons, I found . . . *off-point*. They tended to, I thought, even make fun of us.

Yale defensive tackle, Mick Kleber: There's no question that Garry Trudeau was taking it out on the football players. But we were living such a high life at that particular point that, for me, anyway, I just took it as being good-natured. I just . . . I loved it. I thought it was wonderful. Sometimes he made us out to be kind of stupid, or just sort of frat-type guys that weren't very deep, and you know, I can't say that that's not true in certain cases. But it's very hard to be as deep as Garry Trudeau is, anyway, I would say.

Yale captain and quarterback, Brian Dowling: As a football player the stereotype is conservative . . . right-wing . . . hawk. But that wasn't me . . . so . . .

[Editors note: Forty years later "B.D." remains a character in the Doonesbury comic strip. He has evolved into an ultra-conservative.]

Yale end, Del Marting: Brian is open-minded. He's not...he's not the way he's portrayed. The way "B.D." comes across [in the current strip] is a little heavy.

Yale captain and quarterback, Brian Dowling: . . . but he's got that license to do that in the form of his comic strip. The affinity or the assimilation that I had for the strip when I was at Yale, which was really parodying me and my personality and my publicity, you know we sort of went different ways after school. Although, I think at one time, he had, in the strip, Calvin and me sitting on the bench with the Redskins, and we *were* teammates for a brief time, eight years later. But he took the character in the direction that he wanted to . . . and the similarities obviously ended.

KR (asks Ted Livingston): *Do you still read Doonesbury?*

Yale tackle, Ted Livingston: I do, even though it drives me crazy at times, because I'm. . . . You know, one thing you probably wouldn't ask me, that I'm not sure is very relevant, but for three years I was George Bush's roommate, so, you know. . . . My politics are not one hundred percent aligned with his, but he's a very good friend, and my politics tend in that direction, so I kind of read *Doonesbury* in spite of a lot of what he has to say about the state of the world.

Yale linebacker, Mike Bouscaren: I knew George [Bush] pretty well. We played rugby together, we were classmates at business school, and we went to Maine to see his place . . . and to see my place. . . .

Yale tackle, Ted Livingston: There's a picture of him [Bush] hanging from the goal post in Princeton, in November of 1967 in a, probably, inebriated state.

Yale tackle, George Bass: The Yale football team almost got our president, George Bush, arrested—actually, I think he *was* arrested in Princeton, because he was part of the festivities that was tearing down goal posts, and I believe the police retained him and some other Yale students.

KR (asks Tommy Lee Jones): *You roomed with Al Gore ?*

Harvard guard, Tommy Lee Jones: Yeah.

> **KR:** *What kind of a roommate was Al Gore?*

Funny. We had a lot of fun, probably too much fun. But we got our work done. Everybody did.

> **KR:** *Give me an example.*

Of what?

> **KR:** *Of Al Gore being funny.*

Al Gore

OK. When push button telephones first came in, and we converted from rotary dials to push buttons that made tones, Al was fascinated with it, and the first thing he did was teach himself to play "Dixie" on the tones of the keys . . . and that was rather amusing. I think for a couple of weeks we'd come back to the room and say, "Hey Al, play Dixie," and he'd show us his trick . . . and show the trick to others, visitors. It was funny....

We cooked a turkey in our fireplace one Thanksgiving. . . . We didn't have any place to go. So, we stayed behind for the Thanksgiving vacation and contrived a way to cook a turkey in a fireplace . . .

Yale fullback, Bob Levin: My girlfriend had come . . . from . . . she was at Vassar. Actually, I was dating Meryl Streep at the time. . . .

Yale middle guard, Dick Williams: Well, Bobby Levin and I were in Elihu Club together, and he used to bring Meryl Streep to our dinners on Sunday nights. And I was. . . . In more recent years, I've been amazed by her ability as an actress, because when she used to come to those dinners, she said virtually nothing. Very, very little. Very quiet person. And in those days, there was something of a, how shall I say? . . . Women were sort of to be seen, and not heard. There was this whole thing of women as ornamentation, I guess, something like that, and all of the women's lib stuff was just beginning at that time, but I mean certainly; . . . Meryl Streep . . . no one would ever have known all of that talent lay there.

Yale fullback, Bob Levin: Meryl and I were out on the old campus. We were out putting up "We Won't Go" [to Vietnam] posters, nailing them onto trees, and Brian and his roommates started throwing things at us. They didn't like the idea that we were doing that. That's one of the things I recall, and that was a little bit of a shock, because he was pretty apolitical at the time.

LIFE AT YALE

© 2009 G.B. Trudeau

Yale tackle, Kyle Gee: Yale is a very insulated place and you live in those colleges and you don't have a lot of contact with the out-side world. And Yale was not a hotbed of liberalism at that time period and certainly The Young Americans for Freedom were a more active campus group than, let's say, SDS [Students for a Democratic Society — the largest radical anti-war organization in the country]. And so, we were living kind of an oblivious life and were aware of the outside world, but not really tuned into it that much.

Yale linebacker, Mike Bouscaren: At that age, most people elect-ed not to become involved in politics or social issues. I think those who did were a little more worldly, or you could even say mature…. Yes, I saw that the world was changing. That didn't really affect my day-to-day life as a student at Yale. I followed more conservative guidelines from my parents . . . and was pro-war. . . . If you wanted to find that kind of turmoil, you could, but if you chose just to go to class and play sports, and…. It was never in your face. It never disturbed your day-to-day living. Every now and then there would be. . . . Fifteen guys would go protest in front of some official's office, and it was kind of more of a curious distraction, and most of us told them, you know, "Go hit the books. You're wasting your time."

Yale defensive end, Scott Robinson: My freshman year, there was *one* student with long hair. So, I mean, it changed a lot between then and my senior year, but for the most part, I was pretty . . . most of my friends were pretty middle-of-the-road and relatively conservative.

Yale tackle, Rich Mattas: One of the things, it turns out, I was quite exceptional at doing was drinking beer. And our residential college, on a yearly basis, had a beer drinking contest with our fellow residential college across the street. So, spring senior year, I devoted my training to speed-drinking. They're probably still doing it back at Yale. I haven't checked to find out. But I was one of the people on the team. It's two eight-ounce glasses of beer. Put 'em down as fast as you can, and it's strictly a speed race against the other team.

KR: Do they keep records for this sort of thing?

They do time people. The person—eight people on the team—the last person on line has to drink both glasses one after the other, so clearly, that is the number one position. And, I'm trying to remember who we had as our anchor for that year, but I believe he could put down an eight-ounce glass of beer in under two seconds . . . and it was very impressive.

Yale defensive tackle, Mick Kleber: I remember vividly when birth control first came in. Suddenly, it was like the doors had been flung wide open, and women were much more amenable to just, like, the direct approach. And it seemed like it was very . . . easy. . . . Let me start…let me do this again . . . I can remember very distinctly when birth control came in, and it seemed like the doors were thrown wide open. I'm not saying that's what happened for me and for a lot of the guys that were at Yale. It wasn't like it was a sexual free-for-all or anything like that, but it was certainly, suddenly, much more exciting and the availability . . . the notion that you could meet someone and have sex that evening was on everybody's mind. That's just the way it seemed to be. So, there was a lot of social activity and it was very, very steamy.

THE YALE FOOTBALL TEAM KEEPS
THE FORCES OF REVOLUTION AT BAY

Yale end, Del Marting: Yale's president's office was never occupied. We didn't have the strikes, the protests that they had at Columbia and to some extent, I guess, at Harvard and other places. So, it sounds a little unusual or odd to think, but I believe that the football team's success played a role, not a major role, but a *role* in keeping the Yale campus focused on something other than students' own troubles and worries about Vietnam and all the rest of it.

Yale halfback, Nick Davidson: You had the Tet Offensive and you had the assassinations of Robert Kennedy and Martin Luther King—just these extraordinarily divisive events—and so, in that sense, it [the success of the team] had an amazing healing impact on the community.

Yale end, Bruce Weinstein: I think, given the times, and with us, the country, being at war, it [the team] was something that was easy to celebrate, fun to do, a great release for people, and ultimately, in the big scheme of things, not very important, but, at the time, it was just thrilling . . . a great thing to be a part of.

Yale safety, J.P. Goldsmith: You have to remember it's the '60s. Forget about chronologically: the '60s began with the Gulf of Tonkin Resolution in the summer of '64 and they ended when Nixon resigned. What I mean by the '60s is that everybody had a *mad* on. OK? On strike. Shut it down.

Martin Luther King was assassinated. I'll never forget where I was when that happened. I'll never forget where I was—driving to work to a summer job on the Pennsylvania Railroad—when Robert Kennedy was assassinated. I think that was when the Tet Offensive was and I know it was when Miami and the Siege of Chicago was. OK? So that set the stage. It's the '60s. It's a turbulent time . . . and I want to get back to Hill and Dowling. What I mean about them is this:

You had the *on-strike, let's-shut-it-down* '60s protesters and you had the Wall Street bankers. They didn't want anything to do with each other except on Saturdays in the fall when everybody would call a truce and say *let's see Brian Dowling and Calvin Hill work their magic this week.*

CARM HAS CREATED A FRANKENSTEIN

*Yale's Gallagher brothers
(Fran #77 and Jim #84)
at work against Columbia*

Yale defensive guard, Mick Kleber: We were really used to winning, and we were easy about it. We weren't driven; we were just having a great time. And I think the spirit came into the community when they saw the football team play, and they saw these great plays happen time after time after time and really convincing victories. It just infused everyone with this tremendous sense of . . . *joy.* It was just wonderful to see it, because you knew that. . . . You had a pretty good feeling that you were going to go out there and you would come away with a smile on your face and the rest of the weekend was just going to be a wonderful after-glow.

© 2009 G.B. Trudeau

Yale end, Del Marting: Really thrilling. Things went well, we won the games, we played well, we had great camaraderie. I mean, those things kind of feed on themselves and breed themselves. The more successful we were, the stronger the team became. It just was very graceful, very easy. I mean, when you had a leader like Brian Dowling there was never any question about what we were going to do and how we were going to do it.

Yale captain and quarterback, Brian Dowling: Looking back on the season, I don't think we attempted more than three field goals. We got in the red zone, we scored, or we scored from outside of the red zone. That was my mentality: *you don't settle for field goals.*

Yale end Bruce Weinstein and Yale halfback Calvin Hill

Yale tackle, Tom Peacock: And so as a sophomore, I felt like I was hanging out with giants. You know, you had somebody like Brian Dowling, who was just an absolutely amazing athlete and amazing person. Calvin Hill—and other very talented people who had been playing together. There was a culture on the team of very hard work, discipline, but almost just a casual acceptance that *we're so good and we're going to play really hard and we're going to dominate and we're going to have a great season.*

Yale middle guard, Dick Williams: I used to watch. I have one image in my mind of being on the sideline during a game and watching the offensive line get set. To me, they looked like the Green Bay Packers or something. I mean, I looked out there... they were just professional. You looked at them . . . every guy exactly lined up, their backs exactly the same height. They just looked indomitable.

"They looked like the Green Bay Packers"

Yale captain and quarterback, Brian Dowling: In fact, I think we were in the top five in the country in total offense. Close to 500 yards per game. And at the end of the season the difference between our running yardage and passing yardage was about 100 yards. So it shows the kind of balance we had.

Yale guard, Jack Perkowski: All through that year, I don't think I played in the fourth quarter, because by the time the third quarter was halfway through we were so far ahead that Carm [Yale coach Carmen Cozza] would take out most of the starters to give other people playing time.

Yale safety, J.P. Goldsmith: I don't think the Yale football team of 1968 was ever behind.

Yale tackle, Kyle Gee: I think Bruce Weinstein captured it best. At some point we were playing Dartmouth and things were getting out of hand and Bruce and I were out on the field and Bruce is talking and he said, "You know, it's like Carm has created a Frankenstein, and he doesn't know what to do with it. You know, you just can't stop it. We just keep rolling along and scoring."

Yale cornerback, John Waldman: It was great—winning—but I don't think that we really took on that—I don't know, "air of invincibility" isn't the right thing—the sense that we were doing something special and were really a terrific team until the Dartmouth game, when, I can remember, it was at the Yale Bowl and I think it was full. You know, 56,000 people there, or some huge number of people. And we just blew them away. And I remember looking across—I was standing at the sidelines—looking across the field and the entire Dartmouth team was standing up on the sideline, sort of... with this totally dazed expression on their faces to a man. I mean, it was just odd. And then, we just rolled after that.

Yale tackle, Kyle Gee: I think the focus of every year when I was there was Princeton. You know, I don't really understand all of the roots of it, but if God was going to let you win one game, you'd want it to be Princeton.

    KR: *Not Harvard?*

Not Harvard.

KR (shocked): *Princeton was a bigger deal than Harvard?*

Harvard was this healthy rivalry. Princeton was animus. They were the dark forces in the league the way we looked at it. And as the season rolled on, instead of the focus being on the last game, the focus, in my view, was on Princeton. After we beat Princeton. . . . It wasn't like everybody wrote it off and said the season's over, but everybody's focus, I don't think, was quite as good as it had been up to that point. And that's something that sort of nags at you. You feel like you could have finished it . . . and you didn't.

Yale tackle, George Bass: I remember we were ranked in the top twenty in the country. When's the last time an Ivy League team gets in the top twenty in the country? It didn't happen that often, so it was a big thing. And then the fact that Harvard did so well that year and was undefeated as well. It just pointed to that final showdown.

10

(MEANWHILE AT HARVARD)
WE WERE A REBUILDING YEAR

Harvard center, Ted Skowronski: I think it was viewed as a rebuilding year in every respect. In fact, I remember, I think our very first scrimmage was at the University of New Hampshire . . . and I think we struggled to get a first down. It was that bad.

Harvard cornerback, Mike Ananis: What I recall was that we were chosen for fourth or fifth in the Ivy League. We were not expected to compete for the top. That was going to be for Yale and Princeton and Dartmouth. The pundits—pre-season pundits—selected us to be near the bottom of the Ivy League.

Harvard quarterback, George Lalich: The general thought was—in the press and amongst people you might talk to on the street who followed football—that it might be [Harvard coach] John Yovicsin's first losing year.

Harvard cornerback, John Ignacio: I know that there was a lot of feeling that this wasn't going to be a very good club...but I do know that there were a lot of us seniors who stuck with the program and worked hard and we felt like this was our turn to play. And we wanted to play . . . and we wanted to play well. So, there was that feeling, particularly among the seniors on the team. A lot of us were on defense. You know, we stuck it out. We held dummies . . . and didn't play. We were on the JVs as juniors, and stuff like that, that a lot of folks don't do. And we just wanted to play. And so, there was that kind of emotion behind it. I know I said *what am I doing here? I'm trying to be a baseball player and I'm getting all these injuries. What am I doing?* I said *well, I've gone through all of this. I really want to play.* So, that was, I think, the mentality that a lot of us had.

Harvard center, Ted Skowronski: Just a lot of guys who came up through the ranks, like myself, who had been with the program for three or four years, and weren't stars, but somehow came to fill the positions, through seniority, or whatever, and really, really blossomed.

Harvard captain and halfback, Vic Gatto: When I got elected captain, it was a first ballot thing. I had been the leader—I had been the captain of the freshman team, too—and after that vote, we always go to the Harvard Club of Boston for the post-season dinner. That was the tradition. And at that Harvard Club of Boston dinner, I said, "My class will become the greatest class in Harvard football history . . . and I know none of you sitting here believes it." We'd just come off the '67 season not bad but not great and lost a Yale game that we probably should have won. I don't think anybody, except my own classmates believed me. I don't even think older teammates believed me, because they didn't have the feeling for how outstanding we were as a group. It's just hard to go back and recount it, but boy, we had a talented group of kids, especially on defense.

I had said we're going to go undefeated. Nobody believed me. Nobody thought we were going to be any good. Our coaches didn't think we were going to be good. Yovicsin's statements before the season, frankly, were laughable, in terms of what we knew our ability to be compared to what he'd thought it was.

Harvard captain Vic Gatto

Harvard cornerback, Rick Frisbie: I would say in our case, it was pretty clear that it wasn't the coaches that created that culture and that atmosphere, that it was really the players.

Harvard captain and halfback, Vic Gatto: We wanted to take responsibility ourselves, so we took over the team ourselves. In the spirit of 1968, we took over the dimensions of the team that we could. It still was the coaches' strategies offensively and defensively, but we were responsible for the implementation of that and we took responsibility for it. Early on, coach Yovicsin understood, in a strange way, that he needed to step aside. He had nothing to do with the team, emotionally, and left all of that to us.

Harvard guard, Tommy Lee Jones: John [Yovicsin] was, kind of, a remote man. He was an intellectual when it comes to football.

Harvard coach
John Yovicsin

Harvard cornerback, John Ignacio: Well, Yovicsin was, I always felt, the perfect model for an Ivy League coach. He was very handsome and intellectual looking and he *spoke* intellectually. I mean, I remember we had a fight against Penn and he came in the locker room and he wanted to yell at us for fighting and he said, "Boys, I've told you many times: no *fisticuffs* on the field." He was almost more intellectual than your typical Harvard student. . . . It was more that he was sort of an aloof kind of guy. Didn't really understand the nitty-gritty of the game; he was more into the intellectual writing of an article about the Harvard sweep, or something, rather than knowing about blocking and tackling. Yeah, he was distant. But at the same time, that's the system he set up—that the individual coaches were really your coach.

Harvard defensive end, Pete Hall: What I remember about that was that Vic, elected captain, actually had a meeting and said, we can go through this and just be mediocre and be a typical 6-3 Harvard football team or a 5-4 Harvard football team, but he expected more than that. He wanted us to have a stellar season. So, we went in with some great inspiration from our captain.

Harvard guard, Tommy Lee Jones: We always had team meetings just before the kickoff, where the coaches would leave us alone to ourselves to exchange ideas. Before the first game that we played, Victor Gatto, the captain, spoke. His only thought was to remind us that we had a very good chance to go undefeated. And off we went.

11

PAT CONWAY, VIETNAM, FOOTBALL, AND POLITICS

*Pat Conway arrived at Harvard two years prior to his eventual senior class-
mates. (He dropped out during his junior year, joined the Marine Corps and
served in Vietnam.) Here he begins by describing playing on the freshman
team against Yale on November 22, 1963. . . .*

Harvard safety, Pat Conway: We played down at the Yale
Bowl. The freshmen played on a Friday and that game
started, I think, about noon. We scored two touchdowns
in the first half. *I* scored two touchdowns in the first
half. So we're up like 14-0 and I was back to receive the
opening kickoff for the second half and the referee
comes up to me and says, "Holy cow! Did you hear what
happened?"

And I said, "What are you talking about?"

He said, "The President has just been assassinated!"

And I said, "You're shitting me."

And he said, "No, no."

And I said, "Look, whatever you do, don't tell anybody else, because we want to get this game done
. . . and JFK would have appreciated it if we get
this game done. Keep it under your hat."

At Harvard I had a good athletic career.
I played a number of sports. I
didn't have a good academic
career and I was floundering.
The best thing for me to do
at that time was to leave and
get my head together and
prioritize my life. Vietnam
was raging. I thought I
should do my time in. I have
no idea why I joined the
Marine Corps.

I was sent to Vietnam. Before too long they
sent us to a place called Khe Sanh. And before
my time was over there, they had us surrounded. There
were 5,000 marines. There were anywhere from 25,000
to 35,000 NVA (Northern Vietnamese) and they bombed
us day in and day out. And there are a lot of experiences
I've sort of suppressed.

I left some buddies there. I've been under some incoming that I don't even want to think about. I've had body parts hit my face and hands, you know, flesh. So, those kinds of things you want to put in the back of your mind, but talking about it of late has been OK for me. I can remember landing in California, getting down and kissing the ground. I was so happy to be back. And then, I had my uniform on, I went outside the gate and I get spit on and people threw beer at us when we went to a local bar. Because . . . we were not. . . . It was not a good reception coming back.

Harvard halfback, Jim Reynolds: Pat came back from Vietnam, got the Purple Heart in Khe Sanh and he went up to John Yovicsin and said, "I want to play right halfback." And John said, "Gee, that's going to be difficult, because our captain's there."

Harvard captain and halfback, Vic Gatto: Almost everybody was against the war, including the guys who had been in it, but at the same time we put all those differences aside since clearly Pat had friends that were still in Vietnam. He didn't agree with protesting against *them* . . . and what *they* were doing. . . .

Harvard safety, Pat Conway: So the position of safety was open, and I thought I'd give it a try. Now I *was* a bit of an anomaly. Here I hadn't touched a football in three years, I was twenty-four years old, I was a veteran and I had never played defense at the college level, the varsity level. So, you're talking about a rookie. In fact, that's what they used to call me, the rookie, the oldest rookie in America. But I was so green . . . I didn't even know how to line up on the defense.

Harvard cornerback, John Ignacio: Pat Conway, I felt . . . I kind of revered, because Pat could laugh. . . . Our defensive back coach, Loyal Park, was somebody who was a real taskmaster and overly enthusiastic. But Pat came in from Vietnam, right, and Pat would just laugh at him . . . because he had a whole different perspective. His life wasn't on the line in the jungle and this wasn't a master sergeant, or something, yelling at him. This was just a football coach.

Harvard safety, Pat Conway: My first game of my senior year, coming back from Vietnam, somebody said, "Were you nervous, were you scared, going out on the football field for the first time?" And I looked at him and I said, "Well, you don't get nervous or scared playing a football game. You get nervous or scared being under incoming and live artillery. That makes you nervous or scared. You get excited and enthused about playing football."

Harvard cornerback, Rick Frisbie: Conway was one of the hardest hitters of anyone I knew. Now, fortunately, since I was playing defense, I never got hit by him . . . but I was standing next to him many times or running next to him as I'd see him hit these guys and hear the huge pop. So, Conway was reckless with his body. He was like *I've been through Vietnam. That didn't get me. I can do anything.* I remember plays where Conway would be basically flat-out, parallel to the ground, on his way towards hitting someone.

Harvard defensive tackle, Rick Berne: We used to hang out together and he was older and he had this Vietnam experience and sometimes at night, after a few beers or whatever . . . whatever turned you on . . . we would sit there and he'd tell us some of these stories about Vietnam. And, you know, all of us were against the war at that time— I'd say virtually all of us—but nobody, nobody commented in that way. It was just astounding and he wasn't bragging. It was just another, sort of, feature, another layer that went on, and it was, you know. . . . I think it had a lot do with why we were successful. Everyone was pretty tight, but—genuinely tight, not this nonsense, rah rah stuff. . . .

I participated in the so-called radical politics pretty heavily, along with a few of the guys on the team. I felt you always had to take one side or the other. I took the side of, sort of, the radical side. I can't remember if I joined SDS, but I spent a lot of time with a lot of people in SDS And there's actually a funny story. In our—I think it was our junior year, the year they took over the building—I got called down to the field house to talk to the coaches. . . . And they sat me down and warned me about this communist element I appeared to be involved with and that I might not understand how serious it was and it could affect my life—they didn't say my career as a football player. And I remember sitting there, trying not to laugh. I think at the time, I honestly felt that they had my welfare in mind, but I'll never forget when I got out of there I got everybody together and we had a big laugh about it. So the answer is, I was very involved in it. At least, I felt I was, and I thought it was one of the most valuable experiences while I was at Harvard . . . that whole. . . . I feel very pleased —privileged is too strong—but pleased that I went to school during that era, and I feel sorry for our kids, because I think the environment they are stuck with is not as healthy.

Harvard middle guard, Alex Maclean: Well, I was involved in the anti-war movement, so I was in SDS, with leanings towards Progressive Labor. And I had a lot of friends in SDS, and I participated in anti-war demonstrations, which I don't regret at all. Looking back, I'm quite happy that I did.

Harvard defensive end, Joe McKinney: Alex is sitting there as an SDS member and Conway is over here and here I am with my military uniform going to R.O.T.C. [Reserve Officers' Training Corps] and others who were out there crying about, you know, "ban the war" and everything else. So, it was an interesting time…but we put all that aside . . . we got on the field . . . we were still teammates and we still took care of each other.

Harvard halfback, Jim Reynolds: For me, going through that period of time, where you really, on the Harvard campus, you were challenged. To be a moderate was very, very difficult. They were looking to you— your classmates, your friends, your teachers, people from colleges locally—were looking for you to take a stand. Where do you stand on these issues?

Harvard back-up quarterback, Frank Champi: There was so much going on outside of the world of football, especially in Vietnam and the turmoil that was being created, that I found it very uncomfortable to play a sport and take it all that seriously when people were dying. People my age, people I'd gone to school with, were serving in Vietnam and living in a totally different world than the world I was living in.

Harvard cornerback, John Ignacio: Everything was . . . mixed messages. You know, we were on our Florida baseball trip when King was assassinated. We flew over Atlanta. I'll never forget that. And I was having the greatest time of my life for the first time playing baseball in Florida, and yet, here we were with Martin Luther King. . . . We were watching the flames, watching the fires . . . in Atlanta, and then we landed in Philadelphia to play Penn, and there were flames—we could see them from the sky. So, I had a terrible sense of mixed emotions. My buddies from high school were being killed in Vietnam and I'm out playing football.

Harvard guard, Tommy Lee Jones: It was the best of times and it was the worst of times. Revolution was in the air. People's lives were changing by the minute. Ideas were flying around like bullets. That's kind of what it was like, right?

Harvard safety, Tom Wynne: I recall my junior year, I guess it was, when [Secretary of Defense] Robert McNamara spoke at Harvard. He had spoken somewhere and his motorcade was trying to leave Harvard and that was when hundreds of students just stopped his motorcade. And if I recall, he might have gotten on the back of his vehicle and tried to speak to the crowd. But . . . that just amazed me, that we would do that to a Secretary of Defense. So, it was an eye-opening experience.

Harvard defensive back, Bill Kelly: I wasn't much into politics. I didn't like it. I didn't understand why everyone was so down on the people *fighting* in Vietnam. But I was never into politics. Pretty apolitical. The sexual revolution was there. That was a great time . . . going into Harvard Square and seeing. . . . I think that's when women started to go braless and that was a big thing and sort of an exciting thing back then. Psychedelic music was really different. The drugs . . . I was never into drugs a whole lot, but there was certainly a lot of that sort of stuff.

Harvard cornerback, Neil Hurley: I was at the Pi Eta club the night of the riots in Harvard Square and there was a quarantine going on. I was on the top of the Pi Eta club with a handkerchief over my mouth—because the tear gas was all over the place—and a Budweiser Draft in my hand, watching everything going on in Harvard Square. I mean . . . it was unbelievable.

Harvard guard, Tommy Lee Jones: Because of the war, and because of the strong feeling against it in the community, there was a lot of highly charged political talk going on. Of course, there was the time of the occupation of University Hall, where for the first time in the history of the institution, police from outside of the university had come into *Harvard Yard* and committed acts of violence against undergraduates. That was shaking. One doesn't expect such a thing.

Harvard safety, Pat Conway: When they were closing . . . taking over University Hall . . . they were closing classrooms, they were picketing. The Cliffies and everyone were picketing outside of these classrooms. Honest to God, I used to get up in the morning . . . I used to go to wherever I found a picket line. I used to say, "I'm going into that building. I'm going to class." And they'd try to talk me out of it. I said, "Just move. I'm going in there. If you don't move, I'm going to move you." I'd go into the building, look around, go out the back door, go and find another picket and go right through *that* picket line. And I used to go back to my roommate and say, "I just went to ten classes today that I never even had."

12

BIG HOLE AT QUARTERBACK

Harvard end, Bruce Freeman: We were sort of a rebuilding year, as I remember it, searching for a quarterback.

Harvard quarterback, George Lalich: To be perfectly frank, there were a lot of open positions and holes to fill.

Harvard tackle, Fritz Reed: When we opened training camp *The Boston Globe* had a headline: "HARVARD HAS BIG HOLE AT QUARTERBACK." And George's response at the time was, *"I'm* the quarterback! Who's this guy *Big Hole?"*

Harvard quarterback, George Lalich: I used to like to fool around and make guys laugh and be enthusiastic and include everybody into it . . . whether they're sophomores, juniors, seniors . . . bring everybody in. We're a team. We're a team. I was kind of light-hearted . . . gave that appearance. The fact of the matter is that I was essentially scared out of my mind most of the time . . . I shouldn't say *scared out of my mind* . . . I was nervous . . . but number one: I didn't want to convey that to my teammates, because . . . just *because.* I'm the quarterback, OK? It's just a unique position.

Number two: being light-hearted and having fun and talking and including people and making sure everybody's having a good time helped me deal with the nerves and stress that I had.

Harvard quarterback
George Lalich and
Harvard captain Vic Gatto

Harvard defensive end, Pete Hall: We had some characters on the team that kept us loose. . . . Georgie Lalich, the senior quarterback from Chicago, was absolutely hysterical in calling plays on offense and keeping the team loose. He was just loose. He had a great attitude…the antithesis of a bear-down, in-your-face quarterback. He was the opposite of that. He was low-key; he laughed; he got you laughing; he didn't dwell on mistakes; he had fun…and that rubbed off on the offense.

Harvard back-up quarterback, Frank Champi: I came in fully expecting to be the first-string quarterback. I was playing pretty well in all the pre-season games. In fact, I had a couple people tell me that they thought I probably played better than the first-string quarterback.

However, he was a senior and he had great chemistry with the other players on the team. He was well respected and the coach did, I think, the only right thing to do: you give the senior a chance. And George started the season and the team started winning and it kept winning. He did a great job. You can't argue with success, plain and simple. He did a super job. . . . The team played exceptionally well under his command.

I was the back-up quarterback. All I could do was try to help where I could. I manned the phones. I was the go-between between the backfield coach, who was up high above, and I would relay a lot of information about what was going on during the game. I did the best that I could. I can't say I wasn't frustrated. I was *very* frustrated the whole year. I did not like being the back-up quarterback. I didn't like sitting on the bench. I wanted to be playing, plain and simple. I had lot of pent-up frustration.

13

I REALLY LIKED THOSE GUYS

Harvard guard, Tommy Lee Jones: [Jones, an All-Ivy guard, was the only returning starting lineman on Harvard's offense.] I really liked those guys [his teammates on the offensive line.] I'd say Fritz Reed was one of the most athletic offensive linemen I've ever worked with. Fritz, even as an undergraduate, was interested in commodities. He would call home and check on *pork bellies* . . . and *eggs*.

Harvard tackle, Fritz Reed: I don't think I went there to play football. I went there because I wanted to go to Harvard and football was something I wanted to do there.

Harvard guard, Tommy Lee Jones: Teddy Skowronski was a total workhorse. He got better not only with every game, but with every quarter, and smarter as a football player and always dedicated. He had a brother in professional football and when he finally got a starting job, he had something to live up to...and he did it.

Harvard center, Ted Skowronski: I had a brother who was the co-captain of the Green Bay Packers. So, I was following in those footsteps. He went to Indiana University, and I actually had two other brothers who played football for Indiana University.

KR: So where did all these football genes come from?

That's a very good question. My dad was only about 5'6" and my mom was maybe 5'4", but my grandparents were somewhat larger, so maybe it was generation skipping or whatever. Perhaps the genes came from a lot of hard work, growing up in a factory town. My brother, Bob, was a great player and managed to get a scholarship to Indiana University...starred out there in the Big Ten, was drafted by the Packers and the rest, as they say, is history.

Harvard guard, Tommy Lee Jones: Bobby Jannino was very fast, very quick and also very intelligent.

Harvard guard, Bob Jannino: The team jelled . . . and I think we all genuinely liked each other. We didn't necessarily hang out with each other all the time, but it was a team where there was mutual respect. We were successful, really, because even though we weren't the best athletes, we were all people who were dedicated to doing our jobs and not making others on the team look bad.

Harvard guard, Tommy Lee Jones: Bobby Dowd was the right tackle. He was a junior and matured a great deal that year. He was a little bit green and wide-eyed in the early games.

Harvard tackle, Bob Dowd: My father was a fireman. My mother was a nurse. It was a tremendous thing for them that I was playing football. It was really the only thing I could give back to them . . . pay back to them…and my participation in that game was the biggest thing for my dad and my mother. I could never have given them a better moment after all the work that they did to get me through Harvard.

Harvard guard, Tommy Lee Jones: As a set of offensive linemen, we became more of team each day . . . a smarter team. In terms of . . . if there's any such thing . . . *athletic intelligence* . . . we knew how to learn.

A TRUE TEAM

Harvard back-up quarterback, Frank Champi: I think the reason the team kept winning was that the team had excellent chemistry. I can say that, because I was basically on the outside looking in. I was the back-up quarterback. George Lalich was the first-string quarterback and he had a great rapport with the offense. They were all good friends; they had very strong bonds; they all played well together; and I think probably most importantly, they played as a team, a true team . . . everybody helping out. Nobody was better or thought they were better than the next guy. It was a true team in my opinion.

Harvard defensive tackle, Lonny Kaplan: Because we weren't super-stars we didn't have a lot of egos about who was getting credit for what, but rather we were just doing our job to be successful. I think that really helped us, because people thought of us as just a bunch of average football players . . . but when you put it all together there weren't any weak spots.

Harvard center, Ted Skowronski: It was just something that built week by week. Every victory seemed to bring more confidence, more skill. It was just a team that really, really jelled. I don't think we were extraordinarily talented. We were certainly never as talented as Yale.

GOD THESE GUYS ARE STILL UNDEFEATED

Harvard end, Bruce Freeman: We were thrilled that we were winning, but we were kind of surprised. If you followed *The Boston Globe* in those days, each week it would be: "HARVARD WINS AGAIN" . . . but it was sort of like... the undertone was . . . "*BY SURPRISE, HARVARD WINS AGAIN.*" We didn't think much of it at the beginning of the year. We were just glad we were pulling the team together and that we were having some winning experiences. But as we kept winning, we thought *maybe we're better than we think we are.*

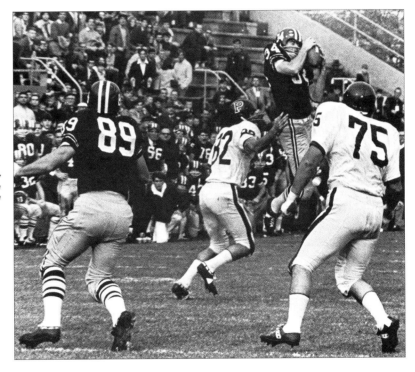

Harvard safety Pat Conway makes his second interception of the afternoon against Penn

Harvard defensive tackle, Lonny Kaplan: Week after week, we surprised more and more people as the season went on . . . you know . . . *god these guys are still undefeated.*

Harvard quarterback, George Lalich: So, everyone's getting more excited, but I think it was the Dartmouth game that really caused people to say *holy smokes! I think these guys are for real.*

Harvard defensive end, John Cramer: We *pounded* Dartmouth. We beat the hell out of them. That's when we realized we really had something because they were kind of our *bête noire*. They were our worst nightmare team, and if we could do well against them, then we figured we could do well against anybody.

Harvard defensive end, Steve Ranere: I think Princeton was the toughest game. It was two weeks before the Yale game. It was down at Princeton. We'd taken an absolute beating from Princeton the year before at our own stadium. It had actually been on TV so it was a little bit embarrassing for us. They were still running the single wing at the time. I think they were the last football team in America to still use the single wing. . . .

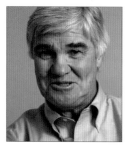

Harvard cornerback, Neil Hurley: Toughest game? Princeton. I can't even remember what the score was, but I remember there was a fourth and one. They were driving for a touchdown, which I think would have put them ahead. And I was playing cornerback, and I didn't make much of a tackle. I grabbled the guy's jersey and Pat Conway came up and just destroyed him. So . . . ball turns over . . . we run out the clock. That was a big win, because you know, the big three: Yale, Dartmouth and Princeton . . . those are important games.

Harvard halfback, Ray Hornblower: I went back to my thirtieth reunion, and the team doctor came up (he must have been eighty-seven . . . he was old) and said, "You know Ray, you had a full cardiac arrest in the Princeton game. You were speared, and we had no pulse for thirty seconds, and if we hadn't converted you, I don't think you would have made it." I got speared right in the chest and it was like someone had hit me with an elephant gun and I was down and out, and someone . . . I don't know whether they converted me through electricity or a punch in the chest . . . but I came back and actually scored the winning touchdown.

Harvard safety, Pat Conway: The toughest. . . . Well, probably the game before the Yale game, Brown, was the toughest game for me because I got a wicked concussion. They had these big running backs and I popped them a few times and I must have softened my head up because one of the last times I hit them, I went dingy. I can remember getting up, going back to the huddle, and something was strange. I'm looking around the stadium and something was just not right . . . and I'm looking . . . and I realize what's wrong. I was seeing in black and white . . . which is a *big* difference. I had no Technicolor in my head. I just lost it.

Harvard end, Pete Varney: Brian Dowling, the quarterback from Yale, hadn't lost a game in college . . . not even in high school had he lost a game. They had Calvin Hill . . . a very prominent running back. They had a stout defense. I think at that time in 1968, Yale was ranked 16th in the country. They were a nationally ranked team. We were definitely the underdog.

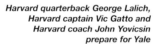

Harvard quarterback George Lalich, Harvard captain Vic Gatto and Harvard coach John Yovicsin prepare for Yale

Harvard defensive end, Steve Ranere: All we were hearing about was Yale, Yale, Yale, Yale. Brian Dowling, Calvin Hill, Weinstein . . . they were terrific. I mean, there's no question: on paper they were a better team than us and they were proving it week in, week out with their wins. But, we were winning our games . . . by not as many points . . . but we kept winning. So, it became . . . it took on its own kind of life . . . and we really believed in ourselves. . . .

16

HOOPLA

Harvard middle guard, Alex MacLean: I think the week before the Yale game, there was just an incredible build-up and swell . . . everything else seemed to drop out. It started with people trying to get tickets to the game. . . .

Harvard linebacker, Dale Neal: It was Harvard and Yale playing each other undefeated for the first time since 1909, I believe. You could have sold 100,000 tickets to this game. I was lucky enough to have eight 50-yard line seats. . . . I could have sold all eight of them for $500 a piece, but I had people that wanted to see the game.

Harvard defensive end, Joe McKinney: I was married. My oldest son had been born in September, and the team had been great in helping us. He had his own jersey. And you know . . . having access to four 50-yard line tickets was a great way to help make ends meet later on in the year. So, I'll just say that. It was anywhere from probably $300 to $500 a ticket.

Harvard defensive end Joe McKinney (#81) with wife Jennifer and baby Joe Jr. To the right is Harvard center Ted Skowronski (#50).

Harvard defensive tackle, Rick Berne:
I rustled up seventeen tickets for that game. And they were going for big numbers . . . as I recall . . . like $500 a ticket or something, which was really big money back then. I remember thinking to myself *I can't believe I'm giving tickets away to all these bums. I could be making. . . .*

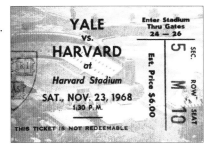

The face-value price of a ticket to the game was six dollars.

Harvard middle guard, Alex MacLean: There was a story every day in the *Globe* about the game, a feature story. So, it really did build as the week went on. It became totally consuming. It was exciting.

> **KR:** *So you might have missed an SDS. meeting or two. . . . ?*

Oh definitely. I don't think they were even happening. That was my impression. The week was focused on the game.

Harvard defensive back, Bill Kelly: If you're on a team like that for a game like that . . . that's all you're thinking about. It's a dream come true to be on a team, undefeated, last game of the year, against another undefeated team. So schoolwork and politics and everything else was thrown to the background. It was just all *game.*

Harvard defensive end, John Cramer: *Boston* got excited. Boston likes winners. They love the Red Sox and so forth. So, they have an undefeated team in their midst and that was something *The Boston Globe* got excited about. The press was all over it. There were reporters at practice every night. Each practice that week was a huge event. It was a very charged atmosphere.

Harvard tackle, Fritz Reed: *Sports Illustrated* was calling into the locker room . . . the amount of hoopla around the game was substantial.

Harvard guard, Tommy Lee Jones: I remember very little about it, but then again, I had my head down. I was usually in the books or in the library or class, and otherwise concerned with keeping up with life in the theatre around that town, which was pretty vital. So, I don't really remember much about the feeling for football around the campus . . . and if I'd seen it . . . if it had become part of my experience . . . I more than likely would have ignored it.

Harvard center, Ted Skowronski: This game meant a lot to me, because I grew up in Derby, Connecticut, only ten miles from the Yale Bowl. As a young boy, as a boy scout, we used to go to the Yale Bowl and watch games. Yale was a huge game for me. Freshman year Yale won something like 45-7. It was an incredible thumping that we took at their hands. We *did* beat them sophomore year [Dowling was injured and didn't play], but in junior year we lost a heart breaker in the Yale Bowl with maybe a minute to go. They made an incredible play. We were going in for a touchdown, and I think we fumbled on the goal line, and they wound up winning the game. We had some scores to settle with them. Perhaps we had a little bit of an inferiority complex with that particular team. I know for myself . . . that's all I read about for years . . . Dowling and Hill.

Harvard captain and halfback, Vic Gatto: They had outstanding talent everywhere. Calvin Hill is going to be the number one draft pick of the Dallas Cowboys. Obviously we're going to struggle shutting *him* down . . . and Brian Dowling was an extraordinary talent . . . as a leader . . . as a quarterback . . . as someone who epitomizes what it means to be a winner.

Yale safety, J.P. Goldsmith: It wasn't just Dowling. If you go by comparative scores, we were better than they were. They had *The Boston Stranglers*, OK? They had a good defense.

Harvard safety, Tom Wynne: All the week of the Harvard-Yale game, a lot was being said about *it's Harvard's defense versus Yale's offense.* We watched films . . . we watched so many films . . . of Brian Dowling just getting loose. It was almost as if no one could stop him. I felt, right before the game, that we had a good enough defense that we could stop him . . . but I was worried.

Yale end, Del Marting: We focused very heavily on the guys on their team. One guy . . . [halfback] Ray Hornblower . . . we were very concerned about. We were impressed with him. It turned out I'd gone to camp with him about ten years before so I knew who he was. I remember Hornblower in camp. He was just a little . . . I wouldn't say a runt . . . but a smaller kid. Very athletic, but. . . . Yeah, he was one we focused on.

© 2009 G. B. Trudeau

Yale guard, Jack Perkowski: That week there was a flu epidemic going around on the Yale campus. Carm and the other coaches were worried about the players getting sick. I seem to remember that about Wednesday—Tuesday or Wednesday—of that week before, they actually moved us out to a motel. So, we stayed in the motel for three nights on the outskirts of New Haven and then went directly to practice.

We were all very focused. We knew it was the last game of the season, and of course, we'd been watching Harvard's progress through the season. Harvard, as I remember, wasn't expected to have much of a team. Every week that we won, we'd look and we saw that Harvard won as well. So we knew we were going into a kind of a showdown where both teams were undefeated.

Harvard center, Ted Skowronski: For the first time in my life . . . my brother having played for Green Bay and being co-captain of the first two Super Bowl teams . . . for once in my life I was playing in the biggest game that week in my family.

Yale linebacker, Mike Bouscaren: The last game you play as a senior is one where there are a lot of conflicting emotions going on that are happening for the first time . . . and, the night before, some of those thoughts were running through my mind. . . .

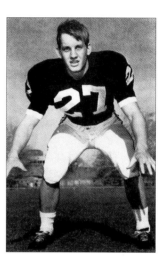

>   **KR:** *What thoughts?*

. . . the thoughts of: *This is going to be my last game. This is going to be my last time I'll wear a football uniform. All of this attention that I've been getting will be gone when I'm just another student.*

*Yale defensive captain
Mike Bouscaren*

Harvard defensive end, Steve Ranere: I think it gave people at the time something to focus on that was good . . . that wasn't controversial . . . that wasn't pitting one against another . . . that wasn't political . . . wasn't religious . . . wasn't social. Here's something we can all feel good about. It's going to be a great day, and for those five or six hours, however long we carried on through the night, it was going to be a time where the world was all peace . . . we're all happy . . . we're all sharing one common goal here, which is to hopefully win this game and have a great afternoon. So, it was exceptional in that. And that's just what did happen.

17

PREDICTIONS

Yale safety, J.P. Goldsmith: It never occurred to us that we were going to lose. It was beyond any wildest dreams that we were going to lose.

Yale end, Bruce Weinstein: Frankly, I'm sure I felt that there was virtually no chance that we could lose.

Yale fullback, Bob Levin: You know I don't even think I thought about the possibility of losing it.

Yale center, Fred Morris: I was confident we were going to win. I wasn't pretty sure, I *knew* we were going to win.

Yale tackle, Tom Peacock: There was never any doubt about what the outcome was going to be. It was just a question of by what margin we would win and what great heroics we would see from some of the key guys on that team.

Yale guard, Brad Lee: I thought it was a pretty sure thing. Looking at the film . . . and I still think this . . . we were three or four touch-downs better than Harvard. I mean the talent gap was significant.

Yale defensive tackle, Fran Gallagher: I don't think there were odds, we were just going to win the game, just like we won all the other games. We didn't think about . . . at least I didn't think about the possibility of losing. I don't think we thought that they were that good. I don't think they were that good. We didn't think we could lose.

Yale defensive end, Jim Gallagher: So their defense was scrappy but our offense was *great*. Scrappy doesn't work too well against Calvin Hill. You better be big and strong and tough.

Yale end, Del Marting: We knew they had a solid team but nothing we'd seen in the films suggested that they were going to have any more success against us than anybody else that we'd played in the last two years.

Yale tackle, Kyle Gee: I'll say this . . . I feel a little embarrassed . . . I'd bought a box of cigars. I brought them up because the guy that coached the line, Seb LaSpina, I knew he liked a cigar and we were going to have a victory cigar. I mean that's not the way you prepare, looking past the game that way.

Harvard end, Bruce Freeman: The night before, you're hopeful and you're really thinking you're kind of invincible. We knew how great Yale was supposed to be but I don't think that deterred any of us. The night before, we thought we've got a chance to beat these guys. We've done great all year. We didn't think we'd be where we are today. You wouldn't think it would be like a miracle. We've won eight games, we've gotten better every game, we can take these guys down. A little bit of bravado, a little bit of arrogance there . . . but you need a little bit of that to win.

Harvard linebacker, Gary Farneti: I was fully aware that on paper Yale had an extraordinary team. It was the classic: "they were big, they were strong, they were fast, they were talented." Other than that they had nothing. We weren't a big team, a fast team, a strong team. We were just undefeated.

Harvard offensive end, Pete Hall: Well I'd seen them on film obviously and I knew how good they were offensively. It was sort of built up as our defense versus their offense. Could we stop Hill and Dowling and Bruce Weinstein and Del Marting, etc. So . . . I was a little bit apprehensive.

Harvard punter, Gary Singleterry: Well, realistically, I guess I felt we were a long shot. You know, we're both undefeated . . . but Brian Dowling was the best quarterback in the league and Calvin Hill was . . . he was a legend. It was hard to imagine beating that team. It really was. So we were definitely the underdog, there's no doubt about it . . . and we knew it.

Harvard cornerback, John Ignacio: Honestly, I thought that we didn't have much of a chance to win at all. I was thinking *how are we going to stop them?* I felt like all we can do is go out and make sure we do our best. I kept saying to myself *I'm going to just tackle really hard, I'm going to really tackle hard, that's my main thing, I'm going to tackle hard, I'm not going to step back, I'm going to go for it and I'm going to really go for it.*

Harvard cornerback, Rick Frisbie: I think that we were foolish enough to believe that we actually had a good chance to win that game. We thought we had a team that was a surprisingly good team that had come this far, that had surprised everyone, including ourselves . . . and we felt that we were really good. We felt that we were far and away the best defense in the Ivy League. We knew they had a great offense but we felt that we could put our defense up against anyone and that we could hold them to twenty points or something and we were pretty confident that our offense could put some points on the board. So we thought we had a really good chance to win the game. I would say that feeling, that I had the night before, didn't last very long into the game.

18

IT WAS A DAY TO PLAY FOOTBALL

Yale captain and quarterback, Brian Dowling: We stayed at the hotel near the end of Memorial Drive, down near the Science Museum. In the morning we got on the busses and we got a police escort. This was the first time I had ever had that happen. And we were driving down the *wrong side* of Memorial Drive . . . police escorted, with motorcycles . . . to get to the stadium. I thought that was really cool.

Harvard defensive end, Pete Hall: It was a beautiful fall day. It was a day to play football. There was a huge crowd. The atmosphere was electric. So . . . the day of the game you couldn't ask for anything better.

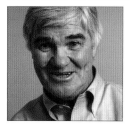

Harvard cornerback, Neil Hurley: I loved playing in Harvard Stadium. The field was unbelievable. It was like playing in the Roman Coliseum. The grass was immaculate, better than any lawn I've ever been able to grow. They never let anybody on it; it was really like a shrine. It was like playing at Wimbledon, only playing football. It was just a beautiful, beautiful place.

Harvard Stadium today

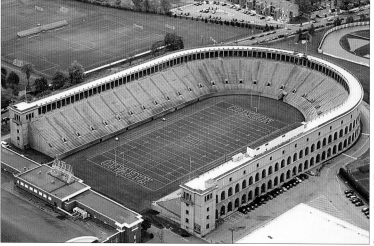

Courtesy http:philip.greenspun.com/

And they played "Ten Thousand Men of Harvard" as you came running out. Every time I hear that song I still think of that.

Harvard Stadium 10 minutes before the game started.

Harvard center, Ted Skowronski: Well, first of all it was a very balmy day which was kind of unusual at Harvard Stadium. Harvard Stadium in November can be extremely cold, extremely windy. I remember it being warm, so *that* was unusual. So the stage was kind of set for something unusual.

Harvard back-up quarterback Frank Champi: My roommate told me that he'd had a dream . . . something to the effect that I was going to get into the game and somehow be instrumental. He said this to me in passing before the game and I just sort of pooh pooh-ed it. But there *was* a strange energy about that day. I know it sounds kind of . . . I don't know what the exact word would be . . . hindsight is 20-20 . . . it's easy to justify something that's already happened . . . but truly there was a strange feeling about that day. It was kind of an *other-worldly* feeling, for lack of a better way of describing it.

Harvard middle guard, Alex MacLean: The stadium was at total capacity. In the whole time I was at Harvard I never saw the stadium so full. It looked like a lot of people must have snuck in or something to fill it so completely . . . the colonnades . . . above the colonnades . . . and it was like a firecracker when something would happen. The roar of the crowd was deafening.

part two

THE GAME

19

YALE WAS HAVING THEIR WAY WITH US

Yale kicks off

Harvard halfback, John Ballantyne: Opening kickoff . . . jitters . . . butterflies. . . . I got the ball, broke to the right. . . .

Ballantyne races to the Harvard 45-yard line

Harvard guard, Tommy Lee Jones: Well, in the early minutes, I remember a great sense of relief that it was finally under way and we could get down to playing football, as opposed to all the things that swirl around playing football.

Six plays later Harvard punts and Yale takes over on their own 14-yard line.

Harvard defensive end, John Cramer: I guess the thing you most remember as a football player is the first set of plays against an opponent. You get a sense about what this opponent is going to be like. I was playing defensive end and I was on the left side, and Yale had these two guys. They had this big tight end named Weinstein and a tackle named Kyle Gee right next to him. They were huge guys . . . and I was *impressed* by them shall we say.

Bruce Weinstein　　*Kyle Gee*

With Brian Dowling in command, Yale begins marching efficiently up the field.

Harvard cornerback, John Ignacio: They just started running the ball right up the field and it was like we couldn't stop them. . . .

Seven plays later Yale has first down on their own 45-yard line. Dowling rolls right, passes, and makes a rare mistake. . . .

Dowling throws

Harvard cornerback, John Ignacio: Then the interception . . . and I was just stunned. He threw it right to me. It was like nobody else was there. I took off down the sideline, and I had this wonderful moment, when I looked straight down the field and nobody was in front of me. I could see the goal line right in front of me down the sideline and I said *oh my god I'm going to score a touchdown.*

Having intercepted Dowling's pass Harvard's John Ignacio flies down the right sideline

That lasted for like a flash of a second . . . and then I got bolted over by a whole bunch of Yalies.

Yale tackle, George Bass: Unfortunately, in the first quarter of the game our quarterback, Brian Dowling, threw an intercepted pass and as I went out to try to tackle the Harvard back who got it, one of them hit me in the knee as it was coming down, and they bent it the wrong direction, and I went down, and they carried me off the field, and that was the last football I ever played.

George Bass

KR: The same thing happened to your replacement.

It was a tough game for left tackles.

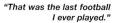

"That was the last football I ever played."

Yale defensive end, Pat Madden: You know, when you lose somebody of his magnitude—he was an incredible player and a major force—that causes us to be less effective than perhaps we would have been, had he been able to play the whole game.

Yale tackle, George Bass: I remember the instant it happened . . . it was a pain unlike any I'd ever felt . . . until I watched my wife have our children. Then I had a feeling of what pain was like . . . except I had it briefly and she had it for many hours. I don't know the name of the truck that hit me and maybe as you do your interviews, you might know the person who remembers putting me down, but I never went back to find out who it was. It wasn't something that I really needed to know.

Harvard cornerback, Rick Frisbie: I'm pretty sure the guy that I hit . . . I don't think he came back into the game. So, you know, I felt like gee, *that was a pretty good hit.* Now I really don't like to . . . thinking back on it . . . I don't really like to think about hitting someone and putting him out of the game, but when you're there on the field, you feel like that's a tremendous accomplishment.

Harvard takes over on the Yale 40-yard line.

Seven plays later they have moved to the Yale 10-yard line. Harvard quarterback George Lalich sprints right, looking to pass.

Harvard quarterback, George Lalich: . . . and I fumbled on the play . . . and I was just totally shocked that I fumbled. Because it wasn't like I was hit hard. It was one of those things where somebody's hand hit the ball out of my arm as I was going down.

Lalich fumbles.

Yale's defensive captain, Mike Bouscaren, recovers the fumble.

Harvard center, Ted Skowronski: That really was a huge turning point for our offensive team, because we came in confident . . . we moved the ball very well early . . . and then had that turnover. . . . And that seemed to turn the tide.

Yale takes over on their own 20-yard line and this time there are no mistakes. Quarterback Brian Dowling, halfback Calvin Hill and end Del Marting put on a dazzling offensive show as they move, in nine plays, to the Harvard 2-yard line.

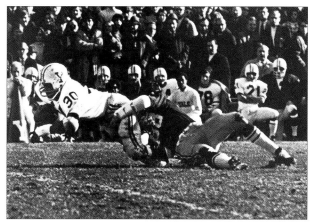

Harvard defensive end Pete Hall tackles Yale halfback Calvin Hill.

The highlight of the drive is a 35-yard run up the middle by Yale halfback Nick Davidson. . . .

Yale halfback, Nick Davidson: At that time my thing was speed off the line . . . I had quite a bit of speed . . . so I got through and I got some daylight. Once I got some daylight I was able to put on some moves and advance the ball, and I was very, very pleased about that. It set up the touchdown.

Nick Davidson

Yale has first down on the Harvard 2-yard line. The Crimson defense digs in. Yale fullback Bob Levin is stopped for no gain. Yale halfback Calvin Hill is stopped for no gain. On third down, Dowling fakes a hand-off to Calvin Hill and races around right end for a touchdown. . . .

Yale quarterback Brian Dowling turns the corner and sprints for the end zone.

Harvard cornerback, John Ignacio: This is the play that I always play over in my mind. It was third and goal on the line, and Dowling ran in for a touchdown. Well, that was my play. I went for the fake to Hill and my real role was to stay put . . . but I couldn't resist. I saw the ball go right into him, so I tried to tackle him, and Dowling took it out and ran around my end. I was beside myself for that because that's a big *no-no* for a cornerback. I talked to Lonny Kaplan after that. He said, "John, they ran over *me* all the way down the field. Don't feel bad."

Three plays later Harvard has the ball on their own 20-yard line. They run a reverse to halfback Ray Hornblower. . . .

Yale middle guard, Dick Williams: I remember one play in particular. You know, the storied running back from Harvard, Ray Hornblower, who had all these legendary moves and was a very elusive runner. . . .

[Editor's note: Ray Hornblower went on to work for five years as a lawyer in the Justice Department and then switched careers and became an opera singer. . . .]

Harvard halfback, Ray Hornblower: From the age of eight I started singing in public, and frankly, singing and running with a football, believe it or not, have a lot in common. Vince Lombardi said you have to run with abandon and you have to play football with abandon . . . and to be a great singer you have to be equally fearless. To cut over a ninety-piece Verdi orchestra with twenty brass takes *cajones*, shall we say, and I just love the adrenal thrill that one gets from singing in public over an orchestra and using my body in almost . . . in a similar way to what a football running back does. You take risks, and you get hooked on the high of taking risks with your body and your "instrument."

On the reverse to Hornblower, Dick Williams flattens him in the backfield.

Yale middle guard, Dick Williams: I remember when I tackled him I stopped him absolutely dead. It was one of these things where it wasn't dragging the ball carrier down. I smacked him absolutely dead. I remember feeling *here is this legendary back . . . the guy must not weigh more than 175 . . .* because it felt like nothing taking him down. I was able to stop him . . . just dead. And to me . . . again, of course, I should hasten to add that he was actually playing injured. So, he wasn't at full speed. . . .

[Hornblower had sprained his ankle badly, the week before, playing against Brown.]

Harvard punts. Yale returns the punt to the Harvard 34-yard line. On first down, Dowling sprints down the right sideline for 14 yards

The first quarter ends with the score Yale 7, Harvard 0.

The Yale cheerleaders suffer a mishap.

Five plays later Yale has fourth down on the Harvard 4-yard line. With characteristic disdain for the field goal option, Brian Dowling decides to go for the touchdown. . . .

Dowling races left, is contained . . .

. . . reverses field with two Harvard linemen in hot pursuit and throws back across the field to . . .

. . . Calvin Hill in the right corner of the end zone for a touchdown.

With this play Calvin Hill breaks the all-time Yale scoring record . . . surpassing the legendary Albie Booth.

[Editor's note: The following year Hill was a first round draft pick for the Dallas Cowboys. He was voted Rookie of the Year in the NFL. Eventually he was inducted into the NFL Hall of Fame. He declined to be interviewed for this project.]

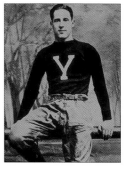

Albie Booth, 1931

Bayliss' extra point kick makes it Yale 14, Harvard 0.

Yale kicks off to Harvard. Speedster John Ballantyne returns the kick-off all the way to the Yale 49-yard line. Four plays later Harvard is forced to punt. The snap from Bob Teske comes back on the ground and Harvard punter Gary Singleterry has to fall on the ball.

Yale now has the ball on the Harvard 37-yard line . . . but fails to make a first down. Yale punter Bob Bayliss kicks a perfect "coffin corner" punt, which goes out of bounds on the Harvard one-yard line.

Harvard can only move the ball out to the 7-yard line and Singleterry is forced to punt again. The snap is good this time but. . . .

Harvard fullback, Gus Crim: Did they block a punt in the first half? That guy came right by me and blocked the punt and I went *jesus criminy should I block this guy?* I mean he was by me . . . I think it was Ed Franklin. . . . Was that the guy? I think that's who it was. Went right by me, blocked the punt, and I said *oh god . . . you can't get a punt blocked . . . you're going to lose.* Because that's what we were always taught: you get a punt blocked on you, and you're going to lose.

Harvard punter, Gary Singleterry: That was the only time in my career at Harvard that I had a punt blocked . . . and I felt like crap.

After Yale defensive back Ed Franklin blocks the punt, causing the ball to fly almost straight up into the air, Yale defensive tackle Tom Neville fields it on a bounce and gets tackled on the Harvard 8-yard line. . . .

On first down, Hill dives forward for three yards.

On second down, from the Harvard 5-yard line....

... Dowling takes the snap ... fakes a hand-off to Davidson ... sprints left ... but is contained by Harvard cornerback Rick Frisbie who chases him all the way back to the 20-yard line. Dowling is now racing to his right, back towards the center of the field, with Frisbie right behind him. Incredibly, in full stride, Dowling now looks back LEFT to the corner of the end zone and throws back across his body to Del Marting for a touchdown.

Dowling sprints left . . .

. . . reverses field with Rick Frisbie chasing him . . .

. . . throws back across his body . . .

. . . to Del Marting who catches it for a touchdown.

After the ref has signalled touchdown Harvard safety Pat Conway . . .

. . . slams Marting to the ground.

Yale end, Del Marting: I scored one touchdown. I remember . . . Pat Conway was guarding me . . . and I caught the pass in the end zone . . . scored . . . and he comes over and out of frustration he throws me down. It was a late hit or whatever you want to call it. You could tell he was frustrated . . . he wasn't panicked . . . but he was annoyed that this was happening and he was going to try to stop it, I guess. I remember looking at him and thinking *come on, Pat . . . get with it.* [Marting and Conway knew each other from prep school, at Exeter.]

Pat Conway

Del Marting

71

Pat Conway (#34) apologizes to Del Marting

Rather than kick an extra point, Yale decides to go for two. Dowling drops back . . . looks left . . . moves leisurely to his right . . . repositions his receivers with a wave of his left arm . . . and completes a short pass—again to Del Marting—for two points.

Score: Yale 22, Harvard 0

Harvard linebacker, Dale Neal: Yale was having their way with us, offensively. They were pretty much unstoppable. So, it was looking pretty bleak when it got to 22-0.

Harvard cornerback, Rick Frisbie: I think that we were a little shell-shocked. I mean, I don't think we could believe what was happening. . . . And the reason it was happening was that these guys were really superior football players.

Harvard defensive back, Bill Kelly: They were going up and down the field and it really did seem like a mismatch. We were just getting whipped all over the field.

Harvard linebacker, Jerry Marino: Well, I don't think we were winning. That was the thing. We weren't doing so well the first half of that game.

Harvard halfback, John Ballantyne: We were getting smoked.

Harvard center, Ted Skowronski: It felt like a tidal wave against us.

Harvard captain and halfback, Vic Gatto: You know, Yale had the ball a lot of the time. They moved extremely well . . . took advantage of a couple of big breaks. . . . Calvin had a big day . . . Brian had a big day . . . and they were just rolling. The first half was difficult for the team and for me, personally. I got hurt on one of the early series. I pulled a hamstring, which I'd had problems with all year, so I'm sort of out of it by that point.

Yale middle guard, Dick Williams: Well, it was business as usual, I would say. I don't know if you know the statistics, but they were net eighteen yards. *Eighteen yards.* That's all Harvard got in the first half. To me that says it all. I mean, we really pretty much shut them down, and we were doing a better job than we actually expected. Now having said that. . . .

Both Hornblower and Vic Gatto, their captain, were not healthy. They spent a lot of time sitting out . . . but even when they were in, they weren't doing much.

Yale middle guard, Milton Puryear: What do I remember from the first half? Just that it was a great day . . . lot of energy . . . we were executing . . . we were doing well. It felt good. It felt really, really good.

Yale center, Fred Morris: *We dominated* Harvard in that first half, and I don't think there was any sense of elation, that somehow we'd gotten out ahead of ourselves. I think it was just a sense of *I'm not surprised . . . we've got a good team . . . we've got a great team . . . we're doing what we're supposed to do. . . .* My recollection of the first half generally is that Harvard wasn't even in the game.

Yale captain and quarterback, Brian Dowling: Well, I seem to recall, it was just sort of business as usual. I think we scored three touchdowns. So. . . . We'd pretty much been on a schedule for the last five or six games, scoring at least one touchdown each quarter. So, I think, business as usual. I was challenged by the fact that Harvard had a good defense, but they weren't going to stop us. We just had too much talent on offense.

Harvard back-up quarterback, Frank Champi: Well, it wasn't going well. I felt for George. He was the starting quarterback. I know what it can be like when things just aren't going right. Vic Gatto, the team captain, and the leading rusher on the team, was injured. Our running game was severely hampered as a result, so Yale focused in on the quarterback, George. They put a lot of pressure on him. They made it very difficult for him.

After their last touchdown Yale attempts an onside kick-off which Harvard recovers on their own 42-yard line. Harvard quarterback George Lalich is unable to make a first down and Harvard is forced to punt yet again.

Five plays later Yale has moved to the Harvard 34-yard line. It is third down and three yards to go. . . .

Dowling takes the snap and pitches left to Calvin Hill. Hill turns the corner. Harvard linebacker Dale Neal slows him down and Harvard safety Pat Conway smacks him hard . . . causing a fumble which is recovered by Harvard tackle Lonnie Kaplan.

In the scramble for the ball, Yale tackle Tom Peacock is injured. Peacock, a sophomore, had replaced injured Yale tackle George Bass in the first quarter. . . .

Hill takes a pitchout from Dowling

Hill turns the corner with Peacock (#68) leading the blocking

Peacock (68) dives for the fumble as two Harvard defenders are about to land on his back

Yale tackle, Tom Peacock: The last play, actually the last play of my football career, was a quick pitch to Calvin. It was a strong side sweep, and as the strong side tackle, the play was set up for me to pull and block down field for him. He got hit—after, of course, he cleared my block, because I threw a good block—and fumbled. I was diving for the fumble, and as I was diving for the fumble, somebody came over the top and hit me in the back. I ended up going into a kind of free-form spasm right there on the field.

Part of my spine was driven into the ground and I was in this kind of odd spasm. They call that a *stinger* . . . where you lose nerve control for a moment.

Peacock's spinal injury is attended to.

I ended up having spinal surgery the summer of 1969 . . . . So, while people were watching Neil Armstrong walk on the moon and cavorting at Woodstock, I was hanging out on a hospital bed in my parents' living room.

Harvard now has the ball on their own 35-yard line. . . .

FRANK CHAMPI ENTERS THE GAME

Harvard quarterback, George Lalich: John Yovicsin did something that surprised me and, I think, a lot of people. He took me out of the game.

Harvard back-up quarterbackback, Frank Champi: Well, coach Yovicsin decided to put me in the game. I was very taken aback by that.

Harvard quarterback, George Lalich: I was very disappointed. I could have played better. I was very disappointed with the substitution...because I was being separated from the guys I'd been playing with all year long...and actually all four years, because so many of us had played together and grown up together in college. Again, that was very disappointing . . . but I understood it one hundred percent.

Harvard fullback, Gus Crim: I remember thinking *George just isn't quite right today . . . just isn't quite right.* Frank came in and I remember thinking I felt so badly for Georgie, because I knew what he was going through. But we needed somebody like Frank.

Harvard center, Ted Skowronski: We *did* need a change. There was just a kind of malaise over the team.

Yale defensive end, Jim Gallagher: It was boring and it was a rout. I mean you're 8-0 and you're in a championship game and you yank your starting quarterback in the first half because he's only completed a couple of passes and you put in a guy that's played what? I don't know. Very little. To me, that's a sign of desperation. . . . I mean they were going nowhere, doing nothing. Our offense was running up and down.

Harvard defensive tackle, Rick Berne: When Champi went in, it was a pretty desperate move by us. I don't think anybody felt he was going to end up being the savior, frankly.

Harvard guard, Tommy Lee Jones: Well, it sort of . . . it looked bad to me. I don't remember feeling really good about seeing that take place, but I was hoping that we could turn Champi's arm to our advantage.

Harvard halfback, Ray Hornblower: Frank Champi was one of the most gifted passers I've ever seen . . . pro or collegiate.

Harvard defensive back, Ken Thomas: He had an arm, let me tell you. He could throw a bullet. He was a little antsy at times . . . a little jumpy at times. But he had an arm.

Harvard end, John Kiernan: Frank could throw a football with either hand. He could throw it eighty yards with his right hand and fifty yards with his left hand. Accurately.

Harvard back-up quarterback, Frank Champi: Well, I taught myself how to throw lefty. I used to be able to throw fifty yards left-handed. I never had to do it in a game, but yeah . . . I used to do that.*

The feeling that I had at the time when I was told that I was going into the game . . . I did . . . I did feel an initial sense of *anger* . . . because I hadn't played much during the year and things weren't going well during the game. Again, I took things personally, especially as a young man. We all. . . . I think the younger you are the more personal . . . the more . . . the more you think things revolve around you, I guess. But I took it very personally. I felt somehow . . . in a strange sort of way . . . that it was a sort of a slight. I don't know. I took it the wrong way.

Harvard halfback, Jim Reynolds: I do have a memory there of Frank . . . when he came into the huddle . . . he was scared to death. He was nervous.

Harvard guard, Tommy Lee Jones: He seemed to be under a great deal of pressure. A little bit nervous at first, I think.

Reed (on left) and Crim

Harvard fullback, Gus Crim: We're on the field . . . we're ready . . . and he walks into the huddle and he calls, "Fawdy wawdy on hut," and everybody kind of looked at each other and I was just *what? . . . what did he say?*

Harvard tackle, Fritz Reed: We had a lot of mid-west kids in there looking at each other.

Champi enters the huddle

* I could throw the football, in those days, as well as anybody . . . and probably further than anybody . . . in the country. I once had a throwing contest with one of the ball players on the team after practice. We were on the 35-yard line, so it was 65 yards to the goal line. He threw the ball. It landed on the goal line. Sixty-five yards. I threw the ball . . . the goal posts were back at the end line, not on the goal line...and the ball went . . . . I threw the ball and it was almost like a perfect throw. It sailed past the goal line . . . sailed through the uprights . . . I'd say it was a good five or ten feet above the goal post and I talked to somebody later who claimed that it went about 90 yards. I don't know. I didn't measure it. I know it went past 75 yards and was still going. Those were the kinds of throws I could make. I could really throw the football in those days and I enjoyed it.

Harvard halfback, Jim Reynolds: But Frank came into the huddle and I think he forgot the play. And he said something like . . . we had these half-huddles . . . we faced the quarterback . . . and I'd be leaning down and Ballantyne or somebody was next to me . . . and Frank called, "Fawdy awdy wawdy," and we all looked at each other and said *holy shit!*

Harvard fullback, Gus Crim: What is "Fawdy wawdy on hut"? And I'll never forget . . . "Fawdy wawdy on hut." "Forty-one on one" was what it was. So we had a little problem acclimating to Frank.

Harvard guard, Tommy Lee Jones: There must have been a communication problem. He was very nervous and his voice was quite tight and he *was* from New England and maybe he didn't . . . maybe his elocution suffered.

Harvard back-up quarterback, Frank Champi: It's possible. I have a Boston accent. I think I had more of one in those days.

But it's possible. Anything is possible. Again, I don't remember the specifics. Whatever they say. . . .

I just wanted to do as well as I could and let the chips fall. I didn't care about winning the game at that point. My feeling was *I'll be damned. I'm not making a fool of myself here.*

And I know it's often said that I was the quiet . . . sort of introverted . . . type and that's true.

That's a big part of me. Amongst people I don't know I am that way. Amongst my friends I never shut up. I'm a totally different person. Again, I was a junior. A lot of the first-teamers were seniors. They didn't know me that well. I was a very introspective quarterback. Whatever.

Harvard defensive end, John Cramer: He was aloof. He was his own person. He didn't really have a lot of friends on the team. . . . Very much a mystery man.

Harvard center, Ted Skowronski: Well, he was a pretty shy fellow. There's no doubt about that.

Harvard halfback, John Ballantyne: I didn't really know him well. I don't want to say a strange guy . . . but certainly didn't quite fit the mold of . . . whatever that means. I'm not sure how happy Frank was being at Harvard.

Harvard defensive end, Steve Ranere: Frank was an individual . . . kind of a loner . . . in a good way. I don't mean that negatively. But he was more into his philosophy, into his own way of life. Not a guy to hang around with the team, go out for beers after a great game, nothing like that.

Harvard punter, Gary Singleterry: Frank was extremely quiet and shy. I think he felt a little out of place at Harvard, to be honest. Harvard can be an intimidating place.

Harvard back-up quarterback, Frank Champi: Freshman year, I actually went out for the baseball team, and sure enough, I was cut. So, I went up to the coach afterwards and I asked him. I said . . . basically, I was really surprised . . . "How can you cut people? All we've been doing is playing catch." He said, "Well, you just don't look like a baseball player." I said, "Oh, OK." I took that at face value. I guess I don't look like a baseball player. I guess I look more like a football player.

Harvard end, Bruce Freeman: I think Frank just didn't look like a football player, when you really get down to it. You know, Rick Frisbie, Gary Farneti, guys like that, they look like football players . . . Pete Varney. . . . Frank didn't look like a football player, but when you ran—

KR: *What did he look like?*

Professor. Linguistics professor. At Harvard.

Frank Champi

Reed (on left) and Crim

Harvard fullback, Gus Crim: Perfect situation for Frank. It was a perfect situation for Frank. There were no expectations. We were getting our butts kicked all over the field and he walked in without any ballyhoo. We always knew he had that kind of talent.

Harvard tackle, Fritz Reed: Yeah, he was a fabulous athlete.

Harvard fullback, Gus Crim: When you can throw the ball with either hand 40 or 50 yards with equal velocity. We knew he had the talent.

Champi enters the game at quarterback with five minutes left in the first half. Harvard trails 22-0. The ball is on the Harvard 36-yard line.

Twelve plays later Champi has moved Harvard to the Yale 15-yard line. The clock shows 44 seconds remaining.

Champi takes the snap . . . pitches the ball to halfback John Ballantyne . . . Ballantyne hands it back to Champi . . . Champi fires a pass left to end Bruce Freeman on the Yale 7-yard line . . . Freeman strides—untouched—into the end zone.

Champi throws . . .

. . . Freeman scores

Harvard back-up quarterback, Frank Champi: That's fun. That's all I remember: a lot of fun. It's always fun to complete a pass. It's even more fun when you throw a touchdown. That's what every quarterback lives for. And I love to throw the ball. I love throwing things . . . baseballs . . . javelins . . . footballs. To this day, I go out in the field and throw the ball. I just love the aesthetics of throwing something and watching it fly.

Harvard lines up to kick the extra point. The snap from Bob Teske is low . . . causing kicker Richie Szaro to miss.

Harvard guard, Tommy Lee Jones: Without blaming anybody, I can't help but think of how everyone's lives would be different if we'd made that extra point. But it takes eleven people to make a mistake.

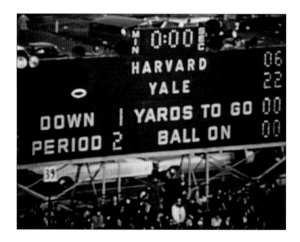

The half ends with the score Yale 22, Harvard 6.

HALFTIME

Yale fullback, Bob Levin: So, I think we went in at halftime pretty cocky . . . although that wasn't characteristic of this team to be cocky . . . but we were confident.

Yale defensive end, Scott Robinson: At halftime, in the locker room, people were throwing oranges at one another around the locker room . . . just messing around . . . screwing around. I mean, it was like *the game is over and . . . yeah . . . we have to go out there for the second half . . . but this is no big deal at all.*

Harvard halfback, Ray Hornblower: There's a very small room where they fit a hundred football players and it's under the stadium stairs. Yovicsin [Harvard coach John Yovicsin] made one more forgettable speech. . . .

Harvard defensive end, Pete Hall: John pleading with us. In his famous halftime speech he'd say something like, "The defense has to hold them, the offense has to score points and the special teams have to execute." Like . . . *OK . . . give me something I can use.*

Harvard end, Bruce Freeman: We were not feeling very good about ourselves, because we were getting our butt kicked. Halftime was a quiet, somber time. I remember Vic and some of the seniors were talking. I don't remember the coach saying much of anything. During the halftime it was more . . . *we need to suck it up and get back out there and show what we can do. . . .*

HARVARD DRAWS CLOSER

On the eighth play of the second half, trailing 22-6, Harvard punts. Mike Bouscaren catches the ball and . . .

Yale linebacker, Mike Bouscaren: The punt that I dropped . . . well I caught it . . . and the ball was stripped out of my hand because I was trying to do something that the coaches told me not to do, which was gain yardage.

Harvard end, Bruce Freeman: I hit the guy with the ball and spun him around and then our guard Bob Jannino hit him . . . after I spun him . . . Jannino just smashed him and I was down on the ground and this ball bounced in front of my facemask and all I had to do was reach out and grab it.

Yale linebacker, Mike Bouscaren: When you do things like that [the fumble] I can't tell you how badly you feel when you go back into the defensive huddle with the other ten guys who are count-ing on you to give them a rest and to catch the ball and do what you're supposed to do . . . and when you make a mistake like that . . . human nature kind of prods you into trying to make it back somehow . . . to do something extraordinary. *That got me into trouble. . . .*

Harvard now has the ball on the Yale 25-yard line. On second down Champi fires a pass to big tight end Pete Varney who pulls it in over his shoulder and bulls his way down to the Yale one-yard line.

**Harvard tight end
Pete Varney on his way
to the Yale one-yard line.**

On the next play fullback Gus Crim dives in for the touchdown.

*Harvard fullback Gus Crim
dives in to the end zone.*

Harvard fullback, Gus Crim: I don't remember much about it. It was just a quick dive, wasn't it?

Harvard guard, Tommy Lee Jones: There was a touchdown scored . . . and if you watch the game films you'll see their defensive lineman . . . go away . . . there was a huge hole there. I was kind of proud of that block.

*Richie Szaro's extra point kick is good and the score is now
Yale 22 . . . Harvard 13.*

HE'D JUST SORT OF MAGICALLY
SLIP AWAY

Two plays later Yale quarterback Brian Dowling demonstrates again his phenomenal scrambling ability in the backfield, evading a total of six Harvard defenders before finally throwing a short pass to Bob Levin. Sportscaster Don Gillis says, "That was a gain of six yards and a run of one hundred and five I think."

Harvard defensive tackle, Lonny Kaplan: I would get past my guy and I'd be in the backfield there and I'd start running after him and, of course, he just was very elusive: he would retreat, he'd change directions . . . and a lot of times we thought we had him hemmed in and he wasn't. I had a sense that I was doing pretty well, one-on-one, with the guy who was blocking me and I was in their backfield a lot but I was never catching Brian Dowling. He got away from everybody.

Harvard end, Bruce Freeman: Dowling reminded me of Fran Tarkington. I mean he really was that kind of a scrambler.

Harvard middle guard, Alex MacLean: Dowling was sort of legendary because he could always slip away when he was in the backfield. On the pass rush you'd feel like you were just about to tackle him and he would elusively evade you . . . which I remember from my freshman year when we played Harvard-Yale. I was playing defensive tackle and I can remember just always almost having my hands on him and he'd just sort of magically slip away. It all happened in slow motion. You could see yourself just sort of floundering after him. That's what it felt like anyway.

Harvard safety, Tom Wynne: I remember being frustrated because I saw Calvin Hill and Brian Dowling, especially Brian Dowling, doing the same things to us that I had seen in the films. They were just running around for so long and we weren't hitting them and stopping them like we had the previous eight games that year.

Yale captain and quarterback, Brian Dowling: It's an awareness of the situation, you know, how long you've been in the pocket—actually I wasn't in the pocket much because the few times I threw from the pocket I'd come off to the sidelines and the offensive coach would say, "If you throw from the pocket . . ." (and I called the plays) ". . . if you throw from the pocket they only have to defend the pass, they don't have to defend you running." So most of my passing was rolling out or sprinting out so that I had the option to run or pass.

But as for scrambling, you know, being competitive you just didn't want to play not *to get something* out of a play. So instead of throwing the ball away I'd continue to look for opportunities, whether to run or pass. I think I had really good balance and good peripheral vision. So those two combined with the competitiveness, I think, ends up. . . . And I had decent speed, probably deceiving, because I have sort of a long stride. It didn't look like I was going as fast as I was. In fact I'm sort of proud of the fact that I had the second fastest 40 [yard dash] time at the Vikings camp. Second fastest *white* guy. So I had pretty decent speed.

Plus, you know, playing with players who understood what I could do . . . Calvin was . . . I never played with anybody in twenty years of playing football who understood scrambling better; maybe because he did it when he was in high school. [Calvin Hill was a quarterback in high school.]

Harvard safety, Pat Conway: The book on Brian was that he threw a soft pass and a little wobbly, as a matter of fact. He didn't have a strong arm. This is what the guys were telling me. Now, I had never played against him. And I'm saying *oh god I'm going to have a great game. I'm going to nail a couple of these balls and I'm going to have the best game of my life* because I was all jacked up. Let me tell you, in the game this guy threw BBs. I mean he didn't float them at all. I was totally impressed with his passing.

CARMEN COZZA

After the scramble, Dowling goes to the sideline to have his legs re-taped and to talk with Yale coach Carmen Cozza.

Harvard halfback, Jim Reynolds: When we used to look at Yale and Cozza, comparing yourself to a *great* coach . . . the players loved him. My cousin . . . I played against my cousin at Yale . . . Jack Ford, who today is in TV and all that stuff . . . but these people *revered* Cozza.

*Yale Coach
Carmen Cozza*

Yale safety, J.P. Goldsmith: Any son or daughter of yours or anybody else's who had a chance to rub shoulders with Carmen Cozza is a better person for it. He's a tough guy, he's an honest guy, an honorable guy and I don't think you're going to see anybody on the team saying anything different. I got a lot more out of Yale football than it ever got out of me . . . and he's one of the main reasons.

YALE KEEPS FUMBLING

Midway through the third quarter Yale faces third down and inches on their own 41-yard line. Fullback Bob Levin dives for the first down and fumbles. . . .

Harvard defensive end, John Cramer: Well, I recovered a fumble . . . and that's about the best thing I did all day. It was a situation where he [Levin] was gang tackled by a group of our defenders and the ball popped loose and it was just sort of . . . there . . . and I kind of . . . pounced on it.

Harvard fails to capitalize on the fumble. Fourteen plays later Yale is driving once again. On first down at the Harvard 35-yard line Calvin Hill takes a pitch left from Dowling, bounces off two Harvard defenders and seems headed for the end zone when Harvard cornerback Rick Frisbie smacks him from behind on the 17-yard line causing a fumble. Harvard safety Tom Wynne recovers on the 10-yard line.

Hill (#30) turns the corner

Livingston (#75) prepares to block Frisbie (top)

Yale tackle, Ted Livingston:
As I recall it was a sweep left, or a pitch left, where I pulled out and was to pick up either the linebacker or the defensive back. I got a sort of a brush block on that guy [Frisbie] but I didn't knock him down, I didn't finish the block and I think he was the guy who, from behind, caused the fumble. So I was there, throwing a block that wasn't the best block it could be but probably was the best block that I had in me at the time. It wasn't from a lack of effort.

I think with any game but particularly with this game and particularly from the Yale side you look back and say *what could you have done differently?* That was one thing that I wish I could have done differently. I don't know if I had the athleticism to do it differently but if I had knocked that guy down there probably wouldn't have been a fumble and we probably would have scored.

Harvard cornerback Rick Frisbie:
I hit him . . . and I hit him where he was carrying the ball . . . and the ball popped out.

[This was the fifth Yale turnover in the game . . . (of a total of seven).]

Harvard defensive end, Steve Ranere:
They were moving up and down the field fairly well. We still really had not controlled them the way we thought we could. They would go for eight, nine, ten-yard runs, they could throw the ball for fifteen or twenty yards but again they would fumble a number of times. And it was those fumbles that were keeping us in the game.

Livingston blocks Frisbie but . . .

. . . Frisbie (#14) stays on his feet and . . .

. . . races after Hill (#30) and . . .

. . . hits him from behind, causing the fumble.

26

SNAKES IN YOUR HEAD

The fourth quarter begins with the score Yale 22, Harvard 13. On the first play of the fourth quarter Harvard's mercurial halfback Ray Hornblower, playing on a weak ankle that he had sprained badly a week earlier, re-injures the ankle after a 6-yard run.

Yale linebacker, Mike Bouscaren: One thing I was very happy about was that I put Ray Hornblower out of the game with a tackle on his bad ankle. You see, all of these people are my friends but Ray Hornblower left my jockstrap on the 10-yard line in the Yale Bowl when we played them our junior year . . . out in the open . . . and that was the first time and the only time that I was ever beat that way. I had a year to think about it and I had a grudge. I was out to get him.

Harvard halfback, Ray Hornblower: I just remember feeling this searing pain in the ankle.

Yale linebacker, Mike Bouscaren: Again, you know, cast in this role of being not skilled enough to play offense, you've got all these snakes in your head about, you know, *I've got to make things happen. I've got to be a bad guy.* And I was really happy to see Hornblower come in to the game . . . and he wasn't in the game for long.

Hornblower is escorted out of the stadium

KR: *So you were the guy? Are you sure you didn't soften him up and someone else made that tackle?*

Yale linebacker, Mike Bouscaren: No, I . . .

KR: *You were the guy who put him out of the game?*

Believe me. I got him with my helmet. You see, I used my helmet like a spear.

[Editor's note: In the movie I show the play a second time and we see that Mike Bouscaren actually didn't make that tackle. Bouscaren has since informed me that he was remembering an earlier tackle that he made on Hornblower in the second quarter, which was followed, several plays later, by Hornblower leaving the game for a while before returning in the third quarter.]

Harvard tackle, Bob Dowd: I mean they [the Yale players] were really joking and laughing and the rest of it . . . so that I was getting angry. I remember a couple of plays in that game where I turned around and made tackles on punts. The first guy I tackled, I didn't tackle him . . . I ran up and grabbed his jersey and I whipped him around and threw him on the ground. I've never done that in my life but on this occasion I was so angry that I threw him like a calf . . . around and on to the ground. I think it was Bouscaren.

27

DOWLING INTO THE END ZONE . . .
YALE 29, HARVARD 13

With eleven minutes remaining in the game, Brian Dowling has marched Yale to the Harvard 5-yard line. Dowling then fakes to Hill up the middle and sprints right, around the corner and into the end zone.

Yale end, Bruce Weinstein: The last touchdown that we scored, Brian was rolling out and decided to try to run it into the end zone . . . and I may have made one of the best blocks of my Yale career. I think it sprung Brian loose. I've got a picture of it that someone at the *Yale Daily News* sent me.

Gary Farneti gets "knocked for a loop" by Yale's Bruce Weinstein. (#89) as Brian Dowling scores.

Harvard linebacker, Gary Farneti: I do remember one play which I will admit was one of the only two times in my whole career where I got knocked for a loop. It had to do with a tight end for Yale who peeled back. I think his name was Bruce Weinstein. I remember him being a pretty big guy that I was aware of only because if I had to go wide on the play he'd be blocking down. Brian Dowling had broken out and was running wide and I was chasing him and I saw Weinstein peeling back at me and I'm trying to calculate *am I going to get to Dowling before Weinstein gets to me?* I was a step short and a step late and I had no defense. He hit me and I think I flew ten feet in the air. That was one of only two times that I actually got blown out of a play.

Harvard defensive end, Pete Hall: The touchdown that got them to 29 [points] went around my end on the Yale side of the field. I just remember looking up and the Yale fans were pointing at me, laughing at me, having a great time and I remember how mad I was and how angry I was.

Harvard safety, Tom Wynne: I remember them scoring down in the open end of the end zone, on the Yale side, and I remember just not being able to get there fast enough. And I remember all the rolls of toilet paper coming out of the stands and I remember one hitting me or coming across my arm and it was just humiliating. I was sitting there thinking *he* [Dowling] *was doing to us what we had watched him do on film. Why can't we stop this guy? We knew he was going to do it.*

Yale place-kicker Bob Bayliss kicks the extra point making the score Yale 29, Harvard 13.

Harvard cornerback, Neil Hurley: I'm attempting to block the extra point. I dive. When I dive my chin strap comes off and my helmet comes off a little bit and my other cornerback, who I think was Rick Frisbie, knees me in the temple. So I get knocked out. I literally lose consciousness. I've seen it on the replay. I'm trying to get back up because I was always taught the old-fashioned way: you get back up, you don't stay on the field. So, I look like a punch drunk . . . getting up . . . then falling down . . . getting up . . . then falling down.

Neil Hurley is carried off the field.

28

THAT WAS AN OMEN

Three plays later Harvard has second down and inches to go on their own 31-yard line. Champi throws long . . . incomplete. On third down he tries a quarterback sneak for no gain. Faced with fourth and inches Harvard decides to gamble. Champi sneaks again and fails again.

Harvard back-up quarterback, Frank Champi: Maybe I didn't put my head down and push hard enough. It was somewhat disappointing. There's no question, I should have made a first down with just inches to go.

Yale takes over on downs at the Harvard 31-yard line. On their second play, with nine minutes remaining in the game, Brian Dowling pitches back to Calvin Hill who then throws a perfect pass to Nick Davidson in the end zone. Harvard safety Tom Wynne bats it away at the last second.

Harvard safety, Tom Wynne: I remember flying over and leaping and getting there just in time to slap it down.

Harvard linebacker, Dale Neal:
Dowling pitched to Hill who then threw a pass and I was the left linebacker and I came around and I just nailed Hill going full speed just as he threw the football. I'll never forget that. I'll never forget the look on his face.

*Hill passes as Neal
(center) is about to hit him*

In the aftermath of the play Yale fans are stunned to see both Dowling and Hill lying motionless on the ground in the backfield. . . .

Yale linebacker, Mike Bouscaren: There was a point where both Brian and Calvin were laid out on the ground . . . and that was an omen . . . I mean, not just for Garry Trudeau and others who were, you know, wearing Chesterfield coats and watching the game but also for the Yale players to realize that the two magic makers, the two rain makers were down. This could be big trouble. I forget, I think one of them was injured, maybe both had injuries coming into the game. . . .

Both Dowling (on the groung) and Hill are shaken up on the play.

Yale captain and quarterback, Brian Dowling: I had a little bit of a sore foot and I just got it twisted. Calvin . . . I don't know what his injury was but he had been in the infirmary all week. He used to run with his tongue hanging out and he got a bunch of stitches in his tongue—it got infected—the week before against Princeton. So he spent most of that week in the infirmary. So I don't think it was *that*. I think he just got shaken up and we both went down. . . .

Hill leaves the field and a Yale coach . . .

Yale linebacker, Mike Bouscaren: When they were both down on the field it was kind of like being kicked in the gut. You had this sense that this could be something different here going on.

Eventually both Dowling and Hill get back on their feet. Dowling stays in the game. Hill limps towards the sideline. . . .

. . . turns him around and sends him back in.

Harvard linebacker, Dale Neal: Hill went off and they turned him around and said *go back in* . . . and he wobbled back in.

The Yale stands erupt in a roar of approval and begin waving the "white handkerchiefs" for the first time. [It is an Ivy League tradition for the fans of the winning team to wave white handkerchiefs at their counterparts across the way when victory seems to be at hand.]

Yale fails to make a first down. Harvard takes over on downs at their own 29-yard line. Six plays later they punt. With six and a half minutes remaining in the game, Yale begins to march down the field again. . . .

IT LOOKED PRETTY GRIM

Harvard center, Ted Skowronski: Again they were driving and it looked pretty grim at that point. I think everyone was pretty down and had the sense that this wasn't going to be our day.

Harvard guard, Bob Jannino: It started to sink in . . . that this may be out of reach . . . it was just going to be too much of a deficit to overcome. Time was the enemy . . . it was pretty much a lost cause.

Harvard center, Ted Skowronski: Being at Harvard-Yale games when those white hankies come out . . . it was a very painful moment for the losing side and I remember those hankies coming out at that point and being totally, completely dejected . . . because I did think it was over.

With four minutes remaining in the game Dowling throws a long bomb to Hill in the end zone which misses his outstretched fingers by inches.

Harvard defensive end, Pete Hall: They were throwing the ball. The white hankies were out. They were pushing to really rub our noses in it. In retrospect, they should have milked the clock a little more. If they had done that the outcome might have been a little bit different.

YALE FUMBLES AGAIN

On the next play . . .

Yale captain and quarterback, Brian Dowling: With three minutes to go it was 29-13. We were driving. I threw a screen pass to Levin . . .

[. . . who gained eighteen yards to the Harvard 14-yard line . . .]

. . . and he tried to lateral to Calvin. So this would have made it . . . he might have scored . . . it might have been 35-13. . . .

Harvard defensive end, Steve Ranere: Bob Levin had the ball. He'd already gone eighteen yards. He got hit by Pat Conway and Mike Georges and was trying to lateral the ball to Calvin Hill. The ball gets fumbled and the ball is there and I pounce on the ball.

Yale fullback, Bob Levin: We made too many mistakes. We fumbled. I fumbled.

Yale captain and quarterback, Brian Dowling: . . . but he fumbled. That started the comeback. But we lost six fumbles that day.

Dowling (#10) throws a screen pass to Levin (top) who . . .

. . . catches the ball and . . .

. . . takes off down field . . .

Yale fullback, Bob Levin: I remember coming off the field with Calvin . . . both of us running together . . . and Carmen looked at us like *what are you guys doing? Why didn't you . . . ?* and we just sort of shrugged our shoulders thinking *well, it's no big deal, Carm. We're up sixteen with three minutes to play.*

. . . *but* . . .

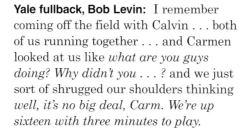

Yale guard, Brad Lee: I just started to get the sense that maybe we had a Greek tragedy unfolding here. Bob Levin was a very tough guy and a very reliable football player and it wasn't like Bob to cough the ball up.

Yale tackle, Kyle Gee: My memory of that game *starts* on that play when we turned the ball over when it was 29-13. That is literally the first play I remember in the game.

. . . *fumbles.*

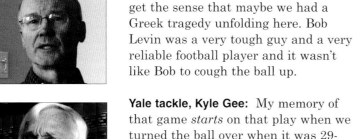

Yale defensive captain and linebacker, Mike Bouscaren: With three minutes to go how bad can you get hurt? My thinking was *you can give up yardage but if you run down the clock . . . that's how you win.*

Harvard safety, Pat Conway: I didn't think at three minutes we had a snowball's chance.

Harvard defensive captain and linebacker, John Emery: I thought *we're down 16 points and there isn't a lot of time* but at the same time . . . you know . . . hope springs eternal, I guess . . . and you're saying *if we could score . . . if we can get a score . . . and then. . . .* So you're just hoping to get that first score and you're really a cheerleader, in that sense, trying to get the offense to get going.

IT LOOKED A LONG WAY DOWN THAT FIELD

After the Yale fumble, Harvard takes over on its own 14-yard line. Three minutes and 34 seconds remain in the game. Harvard trails by 16 points . . . 29-13. . . .

Harvard end, Bruce Freeman: Well it looked a long way down that field. You know a football field is only a hundred yards and when you're playing golf that's a real short shot but I'll tell you when you're standing back there on the 10 or 15 and you're looking to the end that really looks like a long way down there. I think at that point we were saying *OK. One step at a time here, guys. We've got to score. We've got to score as quick as we can and then see what may happen after that.*

Harvard lines up on their own 14-yard line with three and a half minutes leeft in the game.

Harvard tackle, Fritz Reed: I think that's where the attitude was *we've got to remind them that we're still here. We've got to execute. We've got to get this right because we're running out of time. Whether we win or not we're going to remind them that we showed up for the game.*

THE 40-YARD PENALTY

Harvard moves the ball out to its own 29-yard line but then, with two minutes and forty-five seconds remaining in the game, Champi is sacked back on his own 15-yard line.

Champi . . .

. . . is sacked

In the telecast, Harvard captain Vic Gatto—who was injured in the first half—is shown watching from the sidelines as sportscaster Don Gillis says, "There you see captain Vic Gatto . . . a sad ending to his final game as a collegian . . . the outstanding captain. . . .

Harvard captain Vic Gatto (#40), who suffered a hamstring injury in the first quarter watches from the sidelilnes

. . . We have a penalty . . . it's a major from the point of impact which was the 38-yard line . . . brings it out to the 47-yard line [of Yale]. It's a holding."

Yale safety, J.P. Goldsmith: And then, that's when the bizarre things started happening. They called a defensive holding foul on Yale, but they called the penalty from the spot of the foul. Whatever it was it seemed like it was a 40-yard penalty.

Yale defensive end, Jim Gallagher: They're on their 29-yard line. They run their same silly bootleg that wasn't working all day long. I sack Champi—and this seems to be the thread that runs through the final three minutes—I sack Champi . . . he's down on the 15-yard line—*yay yay yay*—I get up and there's some ridiculous flag on the field for somebody holding somebody. Why would you bother holding him? He can't get it to him anyways. It was like a 40-yard gain. Instead of being on their own 15 they're on our side of the field.

Yale linebacker, Mike Bouscaren: I was caught holding someone downfield. This "striper," running along with us downfield . . . you know they don't usually do that . . . and it was away from the play . . . but he calls the holding . . . which was a fair call but I thought it was a little chippy because. . . . Anyway, that gave them a first down and they kept going. . . .

33

THE WHITE HANKIES

Four plays later Harvard has third down and 18 yards to go from the Yale 38-yard line. One minute and thirteen seconds is left in the game. Yale, leading 29-13, inexplicably calls time out.

Harvard tackle, Bob Dowd: I remember the one minute mark more than I do anything else, because at one minute Yale called time out. Now I don't know *why* they called time out. It was foolish. I mean the game was running out . . . we're scrambling from there. During that time out you could see the wave of handkerchiefs waving.

Harvard defensive end, John Kiernan: What I really remember? Those goddamned white handkerchiefs from the Yale side. That I'll never forget. The tradition is you're waving good-bye and basically you're saying to the other side *gee, isn't that too bad. You lost. Oh, what a shame. You lost.*

Harvard linebacker, Jerry Marino: I can remember just getting fired up when those Yale handkerchiefs came out. That *really* fired me up. I was just ready, when I got a chance to get in there, I was ready to do something.

Harvard safety, Pat Conway: I think that's an Ivy League thing . . . waving these white hankies. That's not a good thing to do to the athletes down there . . . wave your hankies at them . . . and if anything ticks you off . . . it's going to make you go at the other team harder or go into the stands and whack a few of *those* idiots. . . .

Harvard halfback, John Ballantyne: The animosity between the Harvard and Yale fans was legendary. Back in those days it's kind of like Red Auerbach smoking his cigar . . . that when you think the game is over you get out these white handkerchiefs and start waving them across the field.

Harvard end, John Kiernan: It means until the fat lady sings, don't wave your white handkerchief. Wait for the final bell or you might eat your handkerchief.

Harvard halfback, John Ballantyne: It was a *sea* of white. It was like, for the most part, this game was over. They were on remote control that this game was in the bag.

Harvard defensive end, John Cramer: I noticed that the Yale fans were getting their hankies out. I noticed that a few fans were starting to leave. It looked all but over. I know my mother, who was watching the game, told me that she was already starting to think of ways to cheer me up.

Harvard cornerback, Mike Ananis: They [the Yale fans] had gone through several choruses of "WE'RE NUMBER ONE" but during that time out it shifted to "YOU'RE NUMBER TWO" . . . one of the few times that I was ever aware of what people in the stands were shouting and I thought for a minute . . . at that moment I thought *no . . . we're not number two. They don't know what a great bunch of guys comprise this team. They don't know the sacrifices that had been made by guys like Pat Conway and Vic Gatto to bring us to this place.*

Yale cheerleaders fire their cannon.

Harvard tackle, Bob Dowd: The Yale band striking up "Mickey Mouse" . . . it's a personal affront to us that, you know, *you're a Mickey Mouse team* and there were flags waving. That created a great incentive in me, and I think everyone, to finish this game . . . that we're not just going to sit down on it. We're going to finish this game.

RUN FRITZ RUN

Time remaining: One minute, 13 seconds

Score: Yale 29, Harvard 13

Harvard ball on Yale 38-yard line. Third down and 18 yards to go.

Yale linebacker, Mike Bouscaren: A Harvard lineman picked the ball up and ran it for 23 yards and half of the people on the Yale defense thought the play was dead . . . and this guy is chewing up yards and going down towards the end zone . . . and finally someone decided it might be a good idea to tackle him.

Frank Champi had dropped back to pass and . . .

Harvard back-up quarterback, Frank Champi: . . . I was about to get hit . . . and I was attempting to lateral the ball . . . this is how I remember it . . . and a Yale defender hit my arm and the ball squirted on the ground and Fritz Reed picked it up and he rambled down the field for significant yardage and a first down. . . .

Fritz Reed (top) picks up the fumble/lateral . . .

Fritz Reed

Harvard tackle, Fritz Reed: Champi was trying to lateral it when he got hit by the guy I was supposed to be blocking . . . so I guess it was a fumble . . . but he was trying to lateral it.

. . . and takes off down field . . .

Yale defensive tackle, Fran Gallagher: Andy Coe and I sacked Champi. After he was down . . . or maybe not—I've never seen film of it—but he threw the ball . . . I thought forward . . . to his tackle who caught it on a bounce and ran with it. Andy Coe looked up at me and said, "He can't do that." And I'm looking and they're doing it. *What's going on here?* Suddenly they're down inside the 10 and now it's going to become a game.

(Run Fritz Run)

Harvard tackle, Fritz Reed: Fran Gallagher was the one who was playing on my head. I blocked him for a while and then he got loose. I can't swear he was the one who caused the fumble but he was by *me* by then. Frank [Champi] was out looking for a place to dump it and he started to lateral and got hit and the ball was on the ground and I picked it up and. . . .

Harvard fullback, Gus Crim: *Run Fritz Run.* That's always in my mind.

. . . to the Yale 15-yard line.

Yale defensive end, Jim Gallagher: Their biggest run of the day was their offensive tackle. They should have put him in there with Gatto.

Fritz Reed

Harvard tackle, Fritz Reed: It's been my position, and it still is, that I led the Ivy League in rushing for average.

Harvard captain and halfback, Vic Gatto: It was one of those times where it's *oh no . . . oh no . . . OH YES!* I mean it was one of those things where you can't believe that something good happened out of a very bad play.

Yale safety, J.P. Goldsmith: It looks like Champi's gone back to pass, it looks like he's trapped . . . he fumbles . . . I don't know . . . and all of a sudden some guy out of nowhere . . . Mister 75 . . . whoever he is . . . he's got he ball!

Harvard tackle, Fritz Reed: It was the first time I'd touched it since I was an end.

Harvard defensive end, John Cramer: Fritz started off as an offensive end and, at the request of the coaching staff, became an offensive tackle and he wasn't terribly happy about that.

Harvard tackle, Fritz Reed: Well, I always viewed playing tight end as the ability to block and sort of be in the line but you also occasionally got to run into the end zone and catch trophies.

Harvard guard, Tommy Lee Jones: Fritz was . . . I remember when they first moved him to offensive tackle—he had been a tight end—and he was outraged and insulted . . . because he wanted to catch passes . . . make what he thought were heroic plays . . . catch passes and run for touchdowns and probably charm the girls by doing it. He somehow felt that he'd been given the job of a *mule* or a *donkey* by going to offensive line and he turned out to be this spectacular athlete at offensive tackle . . . a much better tackle than he was a tight end.

Fritz Reed and Gus Crim

Harvard fullback, Gus Crim: He was moving, I'll tell you that, and I said *just keep running forever with this ball.* I don't know if I just stood there and watched you from behind or....

Harvard tackle, Fritz Reed: My wife has gotten a picture from the TV set and I'm running with it in the picture and you're lying on the ground. . . .

Harvard fullback, Gus Crim: . . . well thank you. . . .

Reed runs as Crim (on ground) watches.

Harvard tackle, Fritz Reed: . . . No, you'd been throwing a block, but you're on the ground looking up. You're in the picture. I'll show it to you sometime.

Fritz Reed and Gus Crim

Harvard fullback, Gus Crim: I just remember seeing your backside and I was never so glad to see your hind side in my life.

Harvard tackle, Fritz Reed: That's a frightening thought.

Harvard fullback, Gus Crim: It *was* frightening . . . but he ran fast and he ran far . . . and that's exactly what we needed.

CHAMPI TO FREEMAN: TOUCHDOWN

Time remaining: One minute.

Score: Yale 29, Harvard 13

Harvard first down on the Yale 15-yard line.

Yale safety, J.P. Goldsmith: And we're, you know, starting to pep each other up in the defensive huddle. But again . . . *no problem . . . we're fine.*

Harvard cornerback, John Ignacio: You know . . . as a kid . . . you always think . . . *we can do it now* . . . and I kept thinking . . . *we can do it now.* . . . And it's sort of a fantasy, you know . . . *oh John . . . you're living in the unreal world* . . . but I thought the grain was there.

Yale tackle, Kyle Gee: I started doing the math in my head, I think, and I said *this might not work out perfectly* . . . you know . . . I can do the math.

Harvard end, John Kiernan: Frank Champi mixed it up as only Frank could do and I think the team was *infused* . . . I mean he was energized . . . the whole team . . . the whole stadium became energized.

Harvard defensive back, Bill Kelly: And *OK OK* . . . you're looking at the clock and you're sort of . . . *we can do this* . . . *something good might happen. Let's score and see what happens.* . . .

Champi receives the snap, drops back and . . .

Champi throws.

Freeman scores.

Harvard end, Bruce Freeman: Frank Champi puts a nice pass in my hands and after that I don't remember. I just remember being in the end zone. . . .

Harvard back-up quarterback, Frank Champi: It was a flood pass. We had several receivers in that area. Bruce was a tall receiver with great hands. I threw a nice pass to him and we scored.

Harvard end, Bruce Freeman: . . . and all of a sudden it's *maybe this thing's possible.* I don't know how much time was left at that point but . . . something around a minute?

KR: *Forty-two seconds.*

Forty-two seconds were left.

INTERFERENCE IN THE END ZONE?

Time remaining: 42 seconds.

Score: Yale 29, Harvard 19

Situation: Extra point. Harvard must go for a two point conversion to have even the remotest chance of tieing the game.

Harvard back-up quarterback, Frank Champi: And then we had to go for the two points. Now *that* I do remember.

Harvard end, Pete Varney: So the formation called for me to split out and I guess the coaches thought there was a physical mismatch . . . not necessarily in speed but in size and bulk . . . and I would run a curl-in and the quarterback would hit me.

Yale defensive tackle, Fran Gallagher: Well, first of all we had a substitute in the game. . . .

Yale cornerback, John Waldman: I was in for exactly *one* play.

Yale guard, Brad Lee: Waldman was probably the smallest player on our team . . . and Varney's large . . . and that's not a good match-up.

Yale cornerback, John Waldman: That was the only play I was in. We were in a goal-line defense, of course, and my job as cornerback was to cover the tight end who happened to weigh about a hundred pounds more than I did and he was about two feet taller than I was.

Harvard end, Pete Varney: I was about 6'2" and probably played at 240 or 245 [pounds].

KR (asks John Waldman): Why would they put you in, in that situation, to cover Pete Varney?

Yale cornerback, John Waldman: Well . . . I guess you'll have to ask the coaches that question . . . I would venture a guess that they thought the game was over. I suspect they wanted to get people into the game so they could say they played in the Yale-Harvard game.

Varney lines up wide left . . . the ball is snapped . . . Champi drops back . . . Varney curls in to the center of the end zone . . . Champi cocks his arm and . . .

Varney lines up wide left.

Waldman covers him.

The ball arrives . . .

. . . and departs.

Yale cornerback, John Waldman: . . . he threw it right at Varney's chest so I just reached around and knocked the ball down. That was the end of the play except that the official called pass interference on it. I have no recollection of touching him whatsoever at all. I've watched the replay about four thousand times and didn't see the pass interference . . . but that's the way it was called.

Harvard end, Pete Varney: I'm sure the Yale person doesn't think it was a good call. I thought it was an *exceptional* call.

Yale defensive tackle, Fran Gallagher: Johnny Waldman . . . I thought he made a *great* play and knocked the ball down and they called pass interference. Now...he went over and kind of around him . . . but it looked very nice, very good to me. I was eight feet away.

Harvard back-up quarterback, Frank Champi: I think, to this day, Yale people will probably claim that that was not interference. That's understandable. Again, that's why we have referees in the game. They call the plays. Without referees nobody would ever get penalized. So I *have to believe* that the referees were correct in their call at that point . . . and thank God they were.

In the aftermath of the interference call, Yale safety J.P. Goldsmith is seen making a highly visible protest . . . kicking the ground, etc. Sportscaster Don Gillis dryly observes, "J.P. does not agree."

Yale safety, J.P. Goldsmith: Upset. I *am* visibly upset. And I'm kicking and making a . . . I was. . . . You know, the first thing I always tell my caddie when I play golf is *please let me behave like an adult.* That was poor form on my part. I don't know if it was interference or not but I was really upset because obviously I didn't think it was interference. . . .

37

I HAD A CHANCE TO BE A HERO

Time remaining: 42 seconds.

Score: Yale 29, Harvard 19

Situation: Extra point. As a result of the interference call in the end zone the ball is moved from the 3-yard line to the 1-yard line and Harvard has another chance to make a two-point conversion.

Harvard cornerback, John Ignacio: On the extra point run when Gus [Harvard fullback Gus Crim] did that, I wanted him to run with Tommy Lee [Harvard guard Tommy Lee Jones] over guard and that's what they did . . . because Tommy Lee was really good. He was an All-Ivy guard. He was very focused. He was a *Texas* football player who knew how to play football more than us New England kind of guys. I thought he would be the perfect guy to run over . . . and they did.

Tommy Lee Jones

Harvard fullback, Gus Crim: So we *have* to score two . . . so that'll probably be me . . . so I just thought *well we're not going to get to this point and not score this...because it does give us a chance to get within a score.*

Yale safety, J.P. Goldsmith: In retrospect, I had a chance to be a hero. I knew in the second attempt at the two-point conversion that their fullback Gus Crim was coming my way . . . and he did . . .

. . . Gus Crim (#30) dives into the end zone . . .

. . . and I whiffed. If ever one had a chance to change the outcome . . . that was it. I knew it was coming . . . and I missed. I was right there. You can look at the film. Either I glance by him or he ran over me . . . or he . . . I was no . . . he. . . . When you talk to *him* he won't mention . . . he won't notice *me* on his way by. I'll tell you that.

Harvard fullback, Gus Crim: Yeah, I don't remember getting hit too much on the thing.

38

THE ONSIDE KICK

Time remaining: Still 42 seconds [The clock doesn't move during extra points.]

Score: Yale 29, Harvard 21

Situation: In order to have any chance of tieing the game, Harvard must somehow regain possession of the ball when they kick off to Yale. On a kick-off, once the ball has traveled ten yards it is anybody's ball. An onside kick is a short, angled kick-off designed to bounce unpredictably and give the kicking team a chance to jump on the ball. It usually doesn't work. . . .

Yale defensive end, Jim Gallagher: So they score and they're down by eight. That's all right. They're kicking off. We'll get the ball. We'll just kneel down or do whatever.

Harvard linebacker, Dale Neal: We knew we were going to onside kick. *Everybody* knew we were going to onside kick . . .

Yale fullback, Bob Levin: An onside kick where everybody in the stands knew they were going to kick it onside except *us.*

Harvard linebacker, Dale Neal: . . . and, amazingly, Yale didn't make any adjustments. I mean they kept their usual line-up of people to receive a kick-off. They had *linemen* in the front row.

Yale defensive tackle, Fran Gallagher: And, of course, we don't have an onside kick play in the return.

Yale defensive end, Jim Gallagher: We had one return team . . . that was it.

Fran (left) and Jim Gallagher

Harvard cornerback, Mike Ananis: Remarkably, Yale was unprepared for this.

Harvard defensive back, Bill Kelly: We had practiced all year an onside kick. It was a situation where Ken Thomas kicks the ball and he kicks it on top of the ball and it will bounce, bounce . . . and then it will take a very *high* bounce.

Harvard defensive back (and onside kicking specialist), Ken Thomas: I'm sitting there knowing, like everybody else in the world, that this is the onside kick. I have to do this. I was terrified.

Harvard cornerback, John Ignacio: Ken Thomas was *really* good at it. He could make the ball bounce, bounce and then make that *high* bounce. He could do that almost all the time.

Harvard defensive back (and onside kicking specialist), Ken Thomas: So now I'm coming off the bench. It was sunny but it was cold and I've got a cold foot and I'm anxious and . . . *hey . . . what are you going to do?...you're the guy . . . you're supposed to do it . . . everybody else knows it's coming. . . .*

Harvard cornerback, Mike Ananis: We looked across the way and there was *number 60* in white shirt with blue number and we just said *number 60 is it* . . . .because we had practiced kicking to a certain place.

Yale guard, Brad Lee (number 60): I knew there was going to be an onside kick. I knew that with a right-footed kicker it was likely to come to my side and I knew, given where I was, that it was likely to come to me.

Yale cornerback, John Waldman: Under the circumstances I'm not sure that you should have *linemen* in the game. And, you know, that's what happened. Brad . . . great guy . . . but he was a *guard.*

Harvard defensive back (and onside kicking specialist), Ken Thomas: I approached the ball and . . . guess what? I *squibbled* it. That famous end-over-ender . . . bounce up into the air . . . it didn't happen. . . .

Ken Thomas kicks the onside kick.

Yale guard, Brad Lee: The ball was heading straight towards me and then it sort of veered . . . just up field. . . .

Brad Lee dives forward for the ball. It bounces off his chest. . . .

Harvard defensive back, Bill Kelly: . . . and then the whole thing slowed down to slow motion. Sort of like if you are ever in an accident, everything just seems to slow down and you can see what's happening. I thought there would be all sorts of turmoil and that people would be smashing into everyone . . . but, as I recall . . . I was just standing there . . . and I saw the ball on the ground . . . and it was just lying there . . . and I said *all I have to do is just fall on this thing* . . .

Kelly

the ball

Lee (#60)

INSTANT REPLAY

. . . and I just fell on it. I had it and got up and gave it to the referee and ran off the field. I couldn't believe how simple it was. A lot of notoriety from just falling on the ground . . . but . . . it was nice.

Yale guard, Brad Lee: Well . . . what happened was the worst possible thing that could have happened . . . so. . . .

YOU JUST GOT THE FEELING THAT THE UNIVERSE HAD SHIFTED SOMEHOW

Harvard linebacker, Dale Neal: Once we recovered that onside kick I just felt that this was inevitable . . . that we were going to go down and score...and somehow get another two points. It had the air of inevitability about it at that point. It had the feeling that we were *destined* to make that comeback.

Harvard punter, Gary Singleterry: At that point I think everybody was so *up*. For the seniors on the team this was their *last hurrah* . . . and they weren't going to blow it.

Harvard tackle, Fritz Reed: We thought we were going to score. At that time we weren't playing, you know, to preserve reputation any more. We thought we were going to score. I think Yale thought we were going to score too.

Yale tackle, Tom Peacock: You just got the feeling that the universe had shifted somehow and that something significant . . . portentous . . . weird . . . was taking place.

Harvard center, Ted Skowronski: You just had the sense it wasn't real. It was happening but . . . yet . . . you couldn't understand why it was happening. . . .

Yale middle guard, Dick Williams: . . . almost like an out-of-body experience where you're watching things happen and you can't believe that it's happening. . . .

Yale end, Bruce Weinstein: I think it was just a slow motion nightmare.

Yale tackle, Tom Peacock: Those last forty-two seconds . . . it really did seem like there was an atmospheric . . . universal . . . some kind of weird force . . . that had descended upon the stadium.

Yale defensive guard, Mick Kleber: I've come to believe that everybody who was in that stadium was sharing the same dream for those final moments. On the Yale side it was a waking nightmare and on the Harvard side it was a miracle but it was the *same dream* for all those people. I tend to believe that that had an influence on the way things worked out because . . . you could cut it with a knife . . . when that was happening. For me it was totally cinematic. It was like looking around the stadium and not hearing anything . . . you know . . . those moments when suddenly . . . all bets are off . . . and you're just on a ride and all you can do is ride it on out.

Yale tackle, Tom Peacock: It just felt like it was meant to be. We were trying to push against fate and fate said *no way guys . . . it's not your time . . . it's theirs.*

40

I JUST FIGURED THIS GUY WAS TOO DANGEROUS TO STAY ON THE FIELD ANYMORE

Time remaining: 42 seconds

[Editor's note: The reader may be wondering why, after the onside kick, there are still 42 seconds remaining in the game. This is a good question. Many Yale people have wondered the same thing over the past forty years. Your editor, who—despite having a father (1942) and grandfather (1903) who played for Yale—attended the game as a Harvard undergraduate, will attempt a possible explanation:

The rule is that the clock starts not when the ball is kicked but when it is first touched, after it is kicked. A close look at the game film reveals that the interval between when Brad Lee first touches the ball and when Bill Kelly falls on it is 35 video frames or 1.17 seconds. It is possible that the timekeeper's finger may have been a tad slow in starting the clock but precisely accurate in stopping it . . . resulting in the clock running for less than a full second . . . and appearing not to move.]

Score: Yale 29, Harvard 21

Situation: Harvard first down on the Yale 49-yard line.

Harvard lines up.

Harvard back-up quarterback, Frank Champi: I was supposed to fade back to pass and look for the open receiver. No receivers were available. . . .

Champi

Dowd   Neville

Harvard tackle, Bob Dowd: Champi's back there, way back there, looking . . . still trying to do something with the ball. Then, that's when Neville [Yale defensive tackle Tom Neville] gets away from me and Champi takes off with Neville chasing him. . . .

Champi scrambles left and turns the corner with Neville in pursuit. . . .

Champi

Neville

Yale defensive tackle, Tom Neville: In the end I felt frustrated because I can remember regularly chasing their quarterback around in the backfield and coming up short. . . .

Champi

Neville

Harvard back-up quarterback, Frank Champi: . . . so I promptly took off and made about fourteen yards. . . .

Champi

Yale linebacker, Mike Bouscaren: It was almost as if the magic that we had become accustomed to, watching Dowling and Hill, had been cast into someone else's capabilities. Who *is* this guy Frank Champi? What's he going to do *next*?

Harvard back-up quarterback, Frank Champi: . . . until I felt my head snap around and a Yale defender was caught for a facemask. Now, I know, to this day, I've heard that they claim it was not a facemask . . . but it sure as heck felt like facemasking . . . a facemask penalty . . . my head whipped around. . . .

Champi

Yale's Mike Bouscaren (#27) commits the foul on Champi.

Bouscaren

Yale captain and quarterback, Brian Dowling: Champi was tackled right in front of our bench . . . and a *late* facemask call . . . I mean it was right in front of us . . . there was no facemask.

Yale linebacker, Mike Bouscaren (#27): I just figured that this guy was too dangerous to stay on the field anymore and that it was my job to put him out. So . . . again . . . trying to make things happen . . . if you try too hard they're not going to happen. But I realized that *here's my shot to get at him* because when you're a linebacker you don't have too many chances to put a quarterback out of the game. He went down before I got to him and when I hit him I got him on the facemask instead of between the facemask and the top of the helmet—which I was aiming for— with a chop. I thought that would do it. But I missed and of course the referees were all over it as he's going down and I got the flag.

Yale linebacker Mike Bouscaren (#27) and Harvard back-up quarterback Frank Champi (also #27) face off as Crim and Ballantyne restrain Champi.

Yale defensive end, Jim Gallagher: Bouscaren said, "Well . . . my hand may have grazed his facemask." As a criminal defense attorney that means *yes I did it.*

Yale linebacker, Mike Bouscaren (#27): My intent was to inflict so much damage on him that he wouldn't be able to play the game anymore. So I didn't care. If I got a facemask penalty and fifteen yards . . . and he can't play anymore . . . that's a good trade as far as I'm concerned. So I was hell bent for destruction and I got what I deserved. Good call.

41

FATE

Time remaining: 32 seconds

Score: Yale 29, Harvard 21

Situation: As a result of Champi's 14 yard run, followed by the 15 yard facemask penalty, Harvard now has first down on the Yale 20-yard line.

Yale safety, J.P. Goldsmith: I don't know whether panic had set in yet but there was certainly *high concern.*

Harvard safety, Tom Wynne: That's when I said *this is magical* and I could see the panic and frustration on the other side. I'm sitting there thinking *we're going to do this* and I felt like they were thinking *yep, they're going to do this.*

Yale linebacker, Andy Coe: A certain element of destiny entered into the game. This was just going to happen the way it ended up happening. This guy Frank Champi comes off the bench . . . he hadn't played all year . . . things just started happening.

Yale defensive end, Pat Madden: It was as if we'd lost control of the game . . . not that Harvard got control . . . but there was some *force* . . . it was a little bit of a hand-of-God kind of issue.

Harvard defensive back, Bill Kelly: You know, things just sort of started . . . going right . . . almost to the point like someone up there was saying *OK, now watch what I'm going to do. I'm going to screw up everything for Yale and they just won't believe what's going to happen to them.*

Yale tackle, Tom Peacock: You just felt there was a script written by a higher power.

Harvard (starting) quarterback, George Lalich: All I know is this railroad train's going and the football gods are saying *you know what? Yale with your white handkerchiefs . . . we're going to teach you a little humility.*

Yale middle guard, Dick Williams: I think, in psychological terms, the supreme confidence that you had has eroded and you can see . . . you can glimpse the future . . . and you say *now wait a minute . . . they actually can score . . . there's a possibility for these guys to actually score . . .* as amazing as that possibility is. At that point you're thinking *oh please don't let them score . . .* as if you needed divine intervention at that point. In other words, you're not relying on your own . . . because it had that sense . . . it had the sense of a Greek play unraveling . . . a tragedy which we all know what the ending is . . . but the players are powerless to stop it.

Yale guard, Brad Lee: The Greek tragedy sense was pretty acute by then. That's all I remember . . . that this seems to be the unrolling of fate. From a Yale perspective it just seemed bizarre.

Harvard (starting) quarterback, George Lalich: You can't even react to it other than to say *holy smoke*. So I had this great enthusiasm for what was going on but at the same time I'm torn by the fact that all these guys who I played with all this time . . . all the way through . . . were out there doing this and I was watching, when I wasn't used to watching. It's like I had been torn away from my brothers.

Harvard cornerback, Rick Frisbie: It's hard to describe the feeling on the bench while you're watching this happen. Up to that point in my life there was nothing that compared to it in terms of the excitement of that last couple of minutes.

> **KR:** *Were you a virgin?*

I was actually just thinking about that. I was not. I was not . . . and I do happen to like members of the opposite sex . . . and that was always something that was very important in the life of a college student . . . but, compared to this, it was nothing.

Yale monster back, Ron Kell: It's almost like . . . here you are . . . say maybe a . . . a prizefighter . . . and maybe you've perhaps *misgauged* something someplace along the line and you realize at the end there that you're in the battle of your life. Yet events kind of snowballed and it happened so very, very quickly.

Yale middle guard, Dick Williams: I had been able to get in [to Harvard's backfield] all through the game but from then on I couldn't get in. I could not get in. No matter what I tried I couldn't get in. I can't explain that.

Yale guard, Brad Lee: Our defense was very good but it wasn't as dominating as our offense was . . . and they had never really had to play sixty minutes before . . . and you had the sense they were getting tired.

Harvard guard, Tommy Lee Jones: I remember telling myself to be cool and stay smooth . . . and *think*. I also remember having the impression that they were getting confused, tired, slow and dumb as the waning minutes went on. I told myself and Teddy [Skowronski] and Bobby [Jannino] that we needed to take advantage of that.

Harvard center, Ted Skowronski: When we were driving for that last score I can remember, being the center . . . always the person who started the huddle and coming out and breaking the huddle . . . I can remember just *floating* to the line . . . literally couldn't even feel my feet . . . tremendous momentum . . . it was as if it was being willed to happen.

Yale safety, J.P. Goldsmith: These guys were playing with happy feet. You've got to give them credit.

Yale defensive tackle, Tom Neville: Some of the offensive stars, Brian and Calvin, wanted to get in *on defense* to stop what was going on.

Yale fullback, Bob Levin: I remember trying to get in [on defense]. I had played monster back my sophomore year. They moved me to offense my junior year. I came up to the [defensive] coach and said, "Let me in. Let me in" . . . because Champi was running around until he found somebody. He was about to let me in but [head coach] Cozza nixed that. He said, "These are the guys we've gone with all year. You're not going in." Brian, too, asked to go in to play some defense and see if we could just get the ball back. But no . . . he wouldn't let that happen, so. . . .

Frank Champi steps up to the line . . . tries to quiet the roar of the Harvard crowd . . . takes the snap . . . flips the ball to halfback John Ballantyne . . . Ballantyne hands it back to Champi . . . Champi fires a long pass to end Bruce Freeman at the 1-yard line . . . Don Martin of Yale breaks up the play.

Time remaining: 26 seconds

Score: Yale 29, Harvard 21

Harvard has second down and ten yards to go on the Yale 20-yard line.

Champi takes the snap . . . drops straight back and throws to Jim Reynolds on the Yale 2-yard line. Again Yale's Don Martin knocks the ball down. . . .

42

THE DRAW PLAY

Time remaining: 20 seconds

Score: Yale 29, Harvard 21

Harvard has third down and ten yards to go on the Yale 20-yard line . . .

Harvard captain and halfback, Vic Gatto: So we're looking for a big play. Pat Stark [Harvard offensive coach] is upstairs talking on the phone and I'm on the phone with him and I'm saying *draw*. We haven't run one . . . not expected . . . definitely not expected with the little amount of time that was left. . . .

Vic Gatto, who was injured in the first half, now re-enters the game . . . limping.

Harvard captain Vic Gatto (#40) who was injured in the first half, re-enters the game.

Harvard cornerback, John Ignacio: And then, when Vic ran out on the field . . . I don't think anybody told him to go out on the field. I think Vic just went out there. My vision was Vic just ran out on the field . . . like . . . *I can't stand this any longer . . . I'm going out there.* I wasn't surprised at all that he ran out there, whether he could run or not. I felt like if there's any way he can do something to win this game . . . he'll do it.

Harvard captain and halfback, Vic Gatto: So we call the draw play to Gus Crim.

Harvard fullback, Gus Crim: When we ran that third down draw . . . both Gallagher brothers [Yale defensive linemen] looped to the outside. It couldn't have been more perfectly done. Both of those guys looped and the thing just kind of opened up and all I could see were the stands. . . .

The Gallagher brothers.

Yale defensive end, Jim Gallagher: . . . and then that run where it looked like we disappeared from the middle of the field. . . .

Harvard fullback Gus Crim (#30) takes off through a gaping hole in the Yale line.

Harvard fullback, Gus Crim: They *read* pass. There's no question they read pass because the first thing I saw . . . and I'll never ever . . . I'll go to my grave seeing those guys loop to the outside . . . and I took off. . . .

Harvard center, Ted Skowronski: We called that draw play. That was so risky. That was a huge play for me because it was run right over my area. I was playing against a very, very gritty opponent, a follow named Dick Williams who was just a very talented player. His great thing was his quickness. He would do a lot of slanting. I remember he slanted one way and I was able to keep my feet and this hole opened up for that particular play.

Yale middle guard, Dick Williams: So they run this play which turns out to be a draw play . . . that I couldn't see developing. I did something hare-brained that I never should have done. My job, when there's a draw play situation, is to guard the middle. In other words, I don't go *anywhere*. You know I was telling you about the "hit-and-read," the "step-around" . . . all of those things that I was doing . . . taking a side . . . going to one side or the other . . . is *not* what you're supposed to do on a draw play. So in my case . . . on this one play . . . God knows why I did it . . . I guess I was trying to make a big play to get Champi and stop it all . . . I actually *took a side* and when that happened I took myself out of the play. When I stepped around to one side their center just isolated me . . . he didn't have to drive block me anywhere . . . all he had to do was just stand between me and the ball carrier . . . and the ball carrier came right up through the middle . . . for something like a fifteen yard gain . . . and then my heart sank. Then I had my heart in my throat. I was thinking *they're actually going to take it down there. They're actually getting down in scoring position.*

Harvard fullback, Gus Crim: . . . and I took off and about inside the 10-yard line I saw two defensive backs converging on me and I said *this is where you hang on* [don't fumble] and I said *maybe I should try to dart around a little bit and maybe I should try to bust one* and then I said *no, maybe I better just hang on to it and if they take me down right here let's go down. Let's not put the ball down* [fumble]. That all went through my mind. And they hit me and I think it ended up on the 6-yard line.

Gus Crim on his way to the Yale 6-yard line.

Harvard immediately calls time out with 14 seconds remaining in the game. The stadium is rocking. . . .

43

PLAYING CATCH WITH MY FATHER

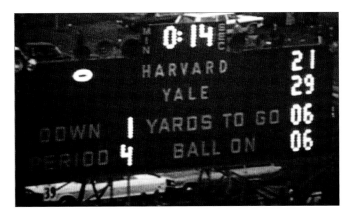

Time remaining: 14 seconds

Score: Yale 29, Harvard 21

Situation: Harvard has first down and goal to go on the Yale 6-yard line.

Harvard has called time out. Frank Champi runs to the sideline to talk to Harvard coach John Yovicsin. He returns to the huddle. Harvard breaks the huddle and lines up. An official waves his arms and intervenes because hundreds of fans have swarmed around the end zone. Police and officials move the fans back a few feet.

A referee moves he fans back.

Harvard lines up again. Champi takes the snap . . . drops straight back to pass . . . looks right . . . sees nobody . . . scrambles left to avoid two Yale rushers . . . tries to run it . . . and gets tackled on the Yale 8-yard line.

Champi looks . . .

. . . scrambles left . . .

. . . and is sacked on the Yale 8-yard line.

Sportscaster, Don Gillis: "The clock is running . . . four seconds . . . three seconds . . . and they stop the clock at three seconds. There will be time for one more play."

Time remaining: 3 seconds

Score: Yale 29, Harvard 21

Situation: Harvard has used its final time out to stop the clock with three seconds remaining in the game. They have the ball on the Yale 8-yard line.

Harvard captain and halfback, Vic Gatto: So now we're down to three seconds and we've got one last play.

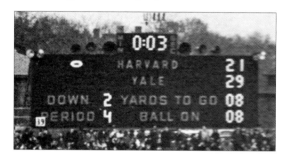

Harvard back-up quarterback, Frank Champi: I called time out. There's three seconds left. We were on the 8-yard line. Yeah, that last play of the game was very strange . . . very surreal indeed. This is pretty much the way it happened:

It was going to be a pass play. I took the ball. I faded back. I couldn't find an open receiver. . . .

Champi lines up . . .

. . . can't find an open receiver . . .

Harvard captain and halfback, Vic Gatto: This time Varney's not open . . . Frank can't see him . . . Varney was clearly the first choice . . . so now Frank's scrambling around. . . .

Harvard back-up quarterback, Frank Champi: . . . I scrambled a little bit . . . did what I could to find some time. . . .

Champi

Neville

. . . and twists away from Yale tackle Tom Neville (#79).

Harvard captain and halfback, Vic Gatto: I started off from the far right hand side and I'm moving my way across the back of the end zone and, you know, I'm not the biggest guy . . . so I've found a way to hide my way across.

Harvard back-up quarterback, Frank Champi: . . . and then there was a very strange thing that happened. Out of the corner of my eye I could see bodies everywhere trying to get to me . . . and then at some point I stopped . . . for like . . . well I'm sure it was just a split second . . . but it seemed like it was almost an eternity. At that point I fully expected to get hit because I couldn't find anybody open. I literally stopped for a split second . . . I was expecting to get hit . . . I was almost at my wit's end . . .and then it was very strange . . . I felt this sense—and again this sounds surreal but I have to relay it the way it happened—I felt almost as if I was encased in an envelope. I felt that nobody could get to me. It was a very strange feeling. I saw these bodies around me but it was almost as if there was a force field around me . . . that nobody was going to get to me. . . .

Harvard captain and halfback, Vic Gatto: Everybody's been pulled across [to the right] with Varney and everybody else, so I end up in the left part of the end zone with nobody around me and I'm signaling to Frank . . . I've got a hand up . . . I'm waving at him. . . .

Harvard back-up quarterback, Frank Champi: . . . so I moved another few steps . . . and, sure enough, I saw Vic in the corner of the end zone, open . . . and it was like a tunnel. There's Vic . . . and Vic is not a very tall receiver but he's the only one I saw and it was almost as if there was a tunnel right to him . . . and I threw the ball. . . .

Champi throws.

Harvard captain and halfback, Vic Gatto: He threw it to me and the ball looked like a watermelon coming at me . . . you know . . . it looked *huge*. It just was that moment where all of those years of playing football and playing catch in the back yard with my father . . . I mean . . . there it was . . . there's that big football coming right at you. . . .

Yale's Jim Gallagher describes the same play:

Yale defensive end, Jim Gallagher: People are within a foot of the field. They're standing all around the end zone and the goal line. They're screaming . . . we're in the huddle . . . and to this day I'm still not sure what defense I was supposed to be in. So I drop back, into that left corner of the end zone . . . Champi is running around back there . . . it seemed like forever . . . I saw him take off to his right—my left—and I start sliding that way five or ten yards . . . and here comes the ball *back* to Gatto where if I had just stayed still and stood there like a statue it probably would have hit me in the helmet. So I suppose I should have been over there. . . .

Harvard's Gus Crim describes the same play:

Harvard fullback, Gus Crim: . . . and all of a sudden here goes this ball . . . and you couldn't see anything because it was in between bodies and everything . . . and there was like a split second in there where it was perfectly quiet. . . .

Vic Gatto catches Frank Champi's pass for a touchdown.

Gatto catches the touchdown pass . . .   *. . . and . . .*   *. . . is mobbed by teammates and fans.*

. . . and then this crescendo of noise started rolling down and it was like somebody put a blanket over you. It was absolutely deafening . . . and here came Vic with the ball and I went *oh my god we scored on that play.*

4 4

WE'RE NOT TIED YET

Harvard fullback, Gus Crim: . . . and the next thing I know, the field is overrun with people. . . .

Hundreds of Harvard fans have poured on to the field in premature *celebration . . . lifting Gatto into the air . . . running wildly in all directions. . . .*

. . . and I'm thinking *my god—we're not tied yet . . . we're not tied* . . . and they've got all these people on the field. . . .

Yale defensive end, Jim Gallagher: There are some more *mature* colleges where their fans are able to resist running on the field . . . especially since you haven't yet even tied the game, let alone won it.

Harvard fullback, Gus Crim: . . . and I'm thinking *this would be the worst thing that ever happened if we can't score these two points.* Now it's serious. Before this we got our butts kicked and we're having a fun time and a couple of breaks went our way. Now it's real serious.

Time remaining: None

Score: Yale 29, Harvard 27

Situation: Extra point. A team is always allowed to go for the extra point (or two points) after a touchdown, even if time has run out. The ball is placed on the three yard line. Harvard, of course, will go for a two point conversion to try to tie the game. There was no overtime in college football in 1968.

Harvard back-up quarterback, Frank Champi: And after *that* . . . we had to go for two points.

Harvard end, Pete Varney: Frank came into the huddle and he looked at me for the extra point and said, "Pete, you really have to get open here. We're going to you." And it wasn't a surprise because we had run that play so many times during the course of the year, successfully, for first downs that I said, "OK. No big deal."

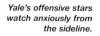

Yale's offensive stars watch anxiously from the sideline.

Harvard back-up quarterback, Frank Champi: At that point—and I think this is true . . . I can say this, I believe, for the rest of the team and hopefully they'll bear me out on this—it was so anticlimactic . . . it was almost like a given that we were going to score two points. I mean I couldn't even *fathom* not scoring two points. I was so certain we were going to get the two points. Again . . . another strange sense of certainty . . . it was as if this had already happened . . . and we were repeating a script of some sort.

So . . . I got the ball . . . faded . . . I did a partial roll to the right. . . .

Champi (bottom) looks for Varney (top).

Yale middle guard, Dick Williams: All I could think was: *no . . . we can't let him throw that ball . . . no . . . he's not going to do it . . .* and he threw the ball. . . .

Harvard back-up quarterback, Frank Champi: Pete Varney . . . very huge and imposing figure that he was . . . I saw him . . . threw the ball. . . .

Harvard cornerback, Mike Ananis: By that time the crowd [at midfield] had spilled on to the field and was twenty deep. I was on the sidelines and couldn't see a thing. I recall turning around, at the 50-yard line, and looking up at the Harvard press box . . . looking at the whole array of stands in front of me . . . waiting . . . and waiting. All eyes were focused at the end of the stadium. Waiting . . . waiting. I knew I'd get a signal, one way or the other. . . .

Harvard end, Pete Varney: He threw it to a place where I don't think I *could* have missed it. . . .

Harvard cornerback, Mike Ananis: . . . and suddenly the entire stadium . . . everything I could see . . . at least twenty thousand of the people who were there . . . hands went up . . . programs, hats went in the air . . . scarves went flying . . . there was an enormous explosion . . . and I knew that we had won.

Harvard back-up quarterback, Frank Champi: . . . he caught it . . . it was very anticlimactic . . . it was just like playing catch at that point. . . .

Varney leaps in celebration

Harvard end, Pete Varney: . . . it really wasn't that great of a catch . . . it was right there . . . like I say . . . if I had missed that one I really would have been like the Bill Buckner of Harvard football history . . . but I did happen to secure it.

Final score: Harvard 29, Yale 29

part three

AFTER THE GAME

45

PANDEMONIUM

Harvard end, Pete Varney: The thought that ran through my mind at the time was that I really wanted to get the ball to Vic Gatto. I wanted him to have it because he was such an inspirational leader, he'd given so much of himself, played hurt that whole game, so I wanted to get the ball to him because he deserved it.

Pete Varney (#80), with the ball in his left hand, races through the crowd looking for Vic Gatto.

Harvard captain and halfback, Vic Gatto: Pete ends up on shoulders. I end up on shoulders. I can see him across still holding the ball. He's trying to get to me to give me the ball. He can't.

Harvard back-up quarterback, Frank Champi: True pandemonium out on the field. I was hoisted on shoulders and Vic was hoisted on shoulders. It was a great feeling, as one could probably imagine.

Harvard linebacker, Gary Farneti: It was bedlam. I never saw a stadium empty so quickly down onto the field in my life.

Harvard tackle, Bob Dowd: I never remember getting hit as hard as I did when that game ended. People came from everywhere and you were like a banana getting hit and squeezed up.

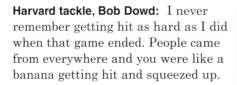

Harvard safety, Pat Conway: I mean people hugging and kissing and, you know, *professors* were coming up to me and hugging and kissing me.

Harvard tackle, Fritz Reed: Right afterwards when people were running out on to the field and little kids were trying to pull the arm pads off for souvenirs . . . just the feeling that it was . . . it was unlike anything I've experienced before or since. It was really exhilarating.

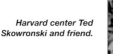

Harvard center Ted Skowronski and friend.

Harvard cornerback, Neil Hurley: Somebody wrote that *Ten Thousand Men of Harvard* were on the field and I think it's true. Just unbelievable . . . fairy tale . . . exciting . . . people coming up to me and asking for my elbow pads and my chin strap and my autograph and of course I still had half vision or double vision from the concussion. My future bride thought I was a celebrity because people were coming up to me and asking for my autograph.

KR: *Did that seal the deal . . . with your wife?*

It sealed the deal. We got married . . . five years later; it took me a little while. She thought . . . her thought when I got knocked out was, "There goes my evening, there goes my date." She didn't know who the hell I was. She didn't know whether I was a waterboy, or what have you, or was I really BS-ing her in terms of was I on the team or not.

Harvard defensive tackle, Lonny Kaplan: My then fiancé, now my wife, was there. She came out on to the field. She found out where I was and I knew where she was and she tells the story that when she came up to me and gave me a big hug and I gave her a big hug I hugged her so hard that I tore the sleeves out of her coat.

Harvard cornerback, Mike Ananis: We were swept up . . . people lifted Harvard players on their shoulders. I can remember getting a glimpse across the way of the Yale sideline and I remember the Yale team standing there . . . white helmets, white shirts, white pants . . . they looked like marble statues. They were frozen in disbelief.

Yale center, Fred Morris: I remember standing on the field and being totally stunned. It was my last college game. It was all over.

Yale monster back, Ron Kell: You know . . . looking up and thinking *is that really it? Is it over?* God, I kept thinking they were going to give us another chance, you know, because it just ended . . . so . . . it just . . . when it was over it was *over*, you know and it was like the stands were just going crazy and people throwing stuff all over the field. I must admit I was very upset that we had lost and would have really liked to have had another chance to do something about it. And . . . you know . . . I'll always remember that stadium and that field. . . .

Yale center, Fred Morris: I remember feeling really alone, surrounded by thousands of Harvard people who were running around screaming and hollering and waving their white handkerchiefs, and thinking *this is surreal. I don't really belong here. I mean, what's going on here? This is ridiculous.*

Yale tackle, Kyle Gee: You know, I'll tell you, I was stunned when it was over. There were a lot of reactions around the side of the field. There was one guy I can remember in particular—I won't say his name—but he was crying like a baby.

Yale safety, J.P. Goldsmith: I don't think there were any tears. It was like . . . *did that just happen?* But again . . . I keep going back to the word *bizarre*. It wasn't painful. It was too strange to be painful.

Yale tackle, Kyle Gee: My reaction was anger. I just felt this sort of undifferentiated anger. I wasn't angry at Harvard. I wasn't angry at the refs. I wasn't angry at *anybody* in particular, but that's what I felt. Anger.

Yale middle guard, Milton Puryear: I think I was in shock . . . defeated . . . just really crushed.

Yale center, Fred Morris: I'm pretty sure it's the same for all of my teammates. For us, it wasn't a tie. It was a loss. It was stunning. It wasn't like we thought *phew . . . man, we got away with a tie.* For us it was like being kicked in the stomach.

Yale defensive back, John Waldman: After the game, you know, it was bedlam. I was upset that we didn't win. I mean we had a great team but, you know, I don't know whether it was rationalization but when I was out on the field and everybody was all mobbing around and screaming and carrying on, I remember thinking *well, you know, if Yale won, it's just another game . . . but this was something special.*

Harvard guard, Tommy Lee Jones: People swarmed around the football field. I simply walked back to Dillon Field House without doing a lot of yelling and running around on the field and making a demonstration of things. I congratulated any of my teammates I could see as I walked back, but my thoughts were rather private. I knew before the game started . . . I was mindful well before the game started . . . well before the *season* started . . . that this game would be the last game of my football career and that I'd really never play the game again and I wanted to be . . . careful . . . and I didn't want to embarrass myself. It was a very private moment for me. I remember being certainly not satisfied with a tie . . . but happy that my career had ended with a team I had a lot of respect for and people that I liked . . . and that we had performed in a way that might be described heroically and acquitted ourselves with honor . . . and that it was time for me to walk back to the field house and put my hat away. So that's what I did.

Harvard fullback, Gus Crim: We were out there for a couple minutes and the crowd thinned out a little and I remember being with Cal Hill. . . .

Harvard tackle, Fritz Reed: Well they came over. They were great sportsmen about it.

Harvard fullback, Gus Crim: They were absolutely great sportsmen but shocked. I remember walking down the track with Cal Hill. And I looked up to him which, of course, you did with Calvin because he was much bigger than they ever had him listed and I said, "Hey. I just want you to know that was a great game. I appreciate the fact that I'm on the same field with you. You're a great athlete." And he looked down at me and he said, "Flah blah nah flah bla na." And I went *what's the deal?* He had bit the end of his tongue off.

[Actually, Calvin Hill had bitten his tongue in the game a week earlier and had received several stitches in it.]

46

IN THE LOCKER ROOMS

Yale middle guard, Dick Williams: There began what seemed like a sort of death march to the locker room.

Yale center, Fred Morris: I remember going back to the locker room. It was dead quiet.

Yale linebacker, Andy Coe: I went in the locker room. I remember crying and feeling really, really bad, you know? Like, this was really an awful experience for all of us and I was really sorry for the seniors and, you know, we had it within our grasp and we couldn't finish the job.

Yale captain and quarterback, Brian Dowling: I think the first thing one of the reporters—you know it was a big thing that I'd played sixty-six games in a row since seventh grade without ever losing a game that I had finished—and I think one of the first questions out of a reporter's mouth in the locker room was, "How does it feel to finally lose a game?" I said, "I thought it was a tie." So . . . that's all I can remember saying in the locker room.

Yale safety, J.P. Goldsmith: It all turns into a blur. One last thing: I played eleven years of organized football . . . from Peewee football in central Pennsylvania to junior high to high school and college. I never used the valuables box. You know, who was ever going to take *my* wallet? OK? I had twenty bucks stolen from me in the Harvard locker room. That was big money. I remember that. They're downstairs celebrating and I'm looking for my twenty dollars. I remember the noise. I can't remember if they were downstairs or upstairs. We had a lot of unopened bottles of Champagne. It was weird.

Harvard captain and halfback, Vic Gatto: It took us a long time to get to the locker room, I'll tell you. I couldn't find . . . we tried to find Calvin and Brian. Calvin was nice enough to come over.

Harvard safety, Pat Conway: In the locker room it was bedlam. Now one good thing is—and my hat's off to him—Calvin came down to our locker room and said good game and stuff like that. That was a real top class thing to do, I mean, they were destroyed and I can understand why they were destroyed but we were just euphoric. There were microphones under us. I must have said a thousand things but I have no idea to this day what I said.

Harvard defensive end, Steve Ranere: Calvin Hill came in. Calvin had come in to talk to Victor, and professional as he turned out to be after that, he did the right thing . . . came in . . . and then Vic actually went in with Calvin to see Brian Dowling to shake hands.

Harvard captain and halfback, Vic Gatto: It was just a wild scene in the locker room. You couldn't hear yourself, the place was packed, you couldn't move. . . .

Harvard defensive end, Steve Ranere: So, once we got in the locker room . . . it's amazing what you think of. You're in so much joy and just appreciating what had happened and you can't believe it, that you've ended the perfect season. But there were people there sensitive to other teammates who were over talking to George [George Lalich, Harvard's starting quarterback who was replaced by Frank Champi late in the second quarter of the game], making sure George felt OK, making sure that he understood that he was part of . . . he got us to where we were. Frank did an outstanding job but George was our quarterback who got us there through that whole year and through that first half of the game and we wanted to make sure that he felt good about that, as hard as it was for him not to be on the field towards the end. So it was joy and tears at the same time.

Harvard (starting) quarterback, George Lalich: We're in the locker room. Everybody's coming in to the locker room and I can hear John Yovicsin, the coach, coming in from the field shouting, "Where's George? Where's George? Where's George?" And he put his arm around me and said, you know, "We wouldn't be here but for you. You had a wonderful year so don't feel bad." And that meant a lot to me . . . that meant a lot to me.

47

LATER THAT EVENING . . .

Yale defensive tackle, Mick Kleber: I remember walking out of the locker room and into the Cambridge night and thinking that Old Blues must be rolling over in their graves and that this game was never going to be forgotten . . . ever. So for me I almost instantly went philosophical on the thing. There was the initial shock of the universe going haywire but after that it came to me, almost like an epiphany, that I was fortunate and everybody who was there at least for those final two minutes . . . I was just so fortunate to have been in that game and to have that experience . . . that I couldn't be sad about it.

Harvard safety, Pat Conway: I got back to my room and there was a big party going on and people jumped up and I'm getting hugged and kissed by girls I never even knew. Some of them very nice, some of them not so nice but I was happy to do that.

Yale tackle, Kyle Gee: My girlfriend at the time knew some people at Harvard and I went to a party in a room at Harvard. People were coming up to me, once they found out who I was, and, you know, trying to be nice, saying, "You guys really were the better team, you probably should have won the game." And it was the very last thing I wanted to hear so I just said, "We've got to hit the road." So we drove back to New Haven and stopped along the way at a diner and had dinner and went on back. So I was back in New Haven by midnight, I guess.

Yale fullback, Bob Levin: We [Levin and his girlfriend Meryl Streep] went to a party at Harvard, believe it or not, and I think we lasted ten minutes . . . it was so uncomfortable . . . and then we just drove back to New Haven . . . the two of us . . . a very long, quiet drive.

KR: Was she into football?

She was, she was very much into football. We had met . . . that was where we had met . . . the first . . . it was actually a blind date and she came up for a football game and was an incredible fan and supporter of it. I just remember it was a very quiet trip. She had an old Nash Rambler. It barely made it back to New Haven. That's what I remember the most . . . the sound of that engine driving down 95 to New Haven.

Yale center, Fred Morris: I remember getting on the bus to go back to New Haven. Dead quiet on the bus.

Yale tackle, Tom Peacock: Young men and older men don't spend a whole lot of time nurturing each other even in a team setting. It was the last game of the season. I remember the bus ride home being one of the most uncomfortable . . . I mean I was physically uncomfortable because of the injury but also psychically. . . . Nobody could say a thing. Everybody was just sitting there in shock. What it felt like to me is that we all kind of hunkered down into ourselves and tried to deal with the inexplicability of what we had just experienced . . . individually.

Yale safety, J.P. Goldsmith: Actually . . . as frustrating as—oh this is stupid—I was going to say that the first time I really slept with my girlfriend . . . I guess she felt so bad for me . . . was when we got back to New Haven.

KR: It took some of the edge off?

It took some of the sting off. Yes it did. New Haven was like a . . . we didn't know how to act . . . it was like a morgue. Now maybe I felt it more than some but . . . the guys . . . we were just sort of staring at each other . . . and again . . . we had a banquet . . . they elected a new captain, Andy Coe . . . and your life goes *on.* . . .

Yale defensive end, Scott Robinson: I think that I had a feeling of disbelief. I didn't believe that it had actually occurred.

In fact I spent the night in Boston that night and got up the next morning and watched a replay of the game on television and I can recall thinking when I was watching that game *that we were going to win.* That's how strong this sense of disbelief was. I carried that with me for a while.

As it turned out it was trumped by another feeling of disbelief. A couple weeks later my father died very unexpectedly. I'm not sure I've ever admitted or told anybody this but I had that same feeling. It was a feeling of disbelief.

Now obviously those are two totally different types of events in one's life but clearly that's how strong that feeling was for me.

Fran (left) and Jim Gallagher.

Yale defensive end, Jim Gallagher: Probably the most upsetting or ridiculous thing was the response of some of the Yale fans to Brad . . . Brad Lee [the Yale guard who failed to recover the onside kick]. He got up there, the ball hits him, he tries to fall on it . . . that's not his fault. You could have had the best hands on the team up there but when you have an onside kick that ball is bouncing around all sorts of places. So you could have had the whole thing stacked up and the same thing could have happened.

KR: *What were the Yale fans doing?*

Yale defensive tackle, Fran Gallagher: They blamed the guy who didn't recover the onside kick, Brad Lee.

Yale defensive end Jim Gallagher: No, not the fans at the game. *Afterwards.* He got hate mail, I heard, you know, *it's his fault because he fumbled.* . . . Here's a guy who's up there blocking . . .

Yale defensive tackle, Fran Gallagher: . . . he's an offensive guard . . .

Yale defensive end, Jim Gallagher: . . . and here's a ball rolling around . . . you know, an onside kick goes really strange . . . and he didn't get it, that's all. That was one of the least . . .

Yale defensive tackle, Fran Gallagher: . . . yeah, to blame him is really silly . . .

Yale defensive end, Jim Gallagher: . . . I mean it was an important play that they got the ball back but there was nothing *he* did wrong.

Yale guard, Brad Lee: The only thing that really miffed me about the aftermath of the game was . . . That night I got the flu and by the time I got back to New Haven the next day I was really sick . . . you know, 103, 104 temperature. I had spent the night in Cambridge with Connie [now his wife] and then had taken a train back to New Haven, feeling worse each mile that the train went. I got in my room, hopped into bed . . . the phone rang. It was a journalist. It was my first serious experience with a journalist. Since then, both teaching at Harvard and working for the military, I've had a lot more experiences so I've learned that this is about par for the course. It was a guy named Leigh Montville who wrote for the *Globe* then and he went on to write for *Sports Illustrated.* He called me up and he had that sort of wise-guy attitude that a lot of Boston journalists have. You could tell that he had a story that he was going to write . . . whatever I said . . . and he was just looking for things that he could grab and twist and make fit the story.

I made a mistake. I was a little bit of a jokester about it. He said, "Well, how do you feel?" You know, basically the question was *Having blown the game, how do you feel for being such a schmuck?*

In a feeble effort to make light of it, with 104 temperature, I said, "I feel lousy. I have the flu." Right. But of course when the story came out that sort of stuff got left out.

I remember him asking me, "What did Hill and Dowling say to you after the game?"

I said, "They didn't say anything to me. There were journalists all over the locker room. It was a madhouse. I just dressed and got out."

He asked, "Did you go back with the team?"

I said, "No. Most of us stayed in Boston that night and went back on our own the next day." That was about it for the interview.

Next day, front page of the *Globe* sports section: *LEE REFUSES TO GO HOME WITH TEAM*, you know, blah blah blah blah.

And then to make it worse, apparently the column got syndicated around the country . . . and telegrams started coming in . . . letters . . . I must have heard from a dozen congressmen . . . a couple senators . . . people from Hawaii . . . maybe a hundred different messages . . . mostly of the ilk that there was some poor guy back in the 1930s in the Rose Bowl who had run the wrong way. I remember one letter said, "Don't worry. He's a very successful insurance agent now" which, at that point, was not terribly reassuring.

That was the one thing that really left a bad taste in my mouth.

THE CELEBRATIONS CONTINUE

Harvard linebacker, Gary Farneti: To say that the partying after the game reached a new level would be an understatement. It pretty much consumed us for the rest of the school year. At the post-season banquets everybody was in a good mood. You could not relive each play too many times. They must have had ten copies of the film because when you run it that many times for the alums . . . I remember when we went down for the post-season banquet in New York at the New York Harvard Club it was the most over-the-top celebration I had ever seen. As a young kid from Binghamton, New York here I am with what seemed like four hundred years of Harvard alums who all showed up for this one. Even after the banquet they had busses that had been rented and reserved to allow the players to go anyplace. The city was our oyster. They had a couple of alums in each bus. I remember we went to nightclubs. . . .

Harvard halfback, John Ballantyne: We had a private party at *The Latin Quarter* and everybody that walked in was asked what kind of bottle of liquor would they like. So they hand us each a bottle of liquor. . . .

Harvard linebacker, Gary Farneti: We had alums paying the tabs. In those days eighteen years old was the legal drinking age in New York. It was not in Massachusetts. We enjoyed ourselves, to say the least. I don't think we got back until three or four in the morning. I thought to myself *if this is what football is like at Harvard, this is a great choice I made*. It didn't occur to me that maybe a game like that is a once-in-a-lifetime event. It wasn't the standard. Not all Yale games are going to be like this . . . but I relished every minute of it. I think for the alums it was the same way. It was just a communal festival. The thing that was most impressive to me was that I was looking at alums at those banquets in their mid to late eighties along with alums who were two years out of college . . . and everything in between . . . as avidly engaged in the celebration as if they had all played on the team. I had never experienced anything like that in my life. I had heard of alumni organizations but those seemed like sterile organizations somewhere out there that do things . . . I'm not sure what. But this was a coming together of anybody and everybody who could possibly get there and it was a once-in-a-lifetime experience both on the field and off. I never saw that again throughout the rest of my Harvard career.

IT KEEPS COMING BACK AT YOU

Harvard captain and halfback, Vic Gatto: It is one of those memories . . . New England sports memories . . . and actually because Harvard and Yale alumni are around the world . . . that keeps coming back at you. I'm sure I've had, you know, many more than Harvard Stadium held . . . eighty thousand people tell me where they were . . . what happened at that game . . . at that time . . . where they were listening to it on the radio or whatever it was . . . because it's one of those memories that you like to think about. It's a happy memory and there was a lot going on [in the country] that wasn't so happy during those years and this was a happy time and a great memory for everybody.

Yale tackle, Kyle Gee: Credit to Harvard. They were there at exactly the right moment and they did all the right things . . . but, you know, I would say that this game probably bothers me to this day. George Allen, who is not a coach that I admire that much . . . but he had this saying that he would use with his players that always struck me as very much over the top: "Every time you lose you die a little." I don't think that's true but I think every time you come from 29-13 to 29-29 you die a little. It took a long time to swallow it. My friends joke that if I had an MRI right now there would be a little lesion up there that reads "29-29."

Harvard back-up quarterback, Frank Champi: I guess I knew that it was going to be my defining moment as an athlete. I didn't expect to top that in whatever I did. I was concerned that it might be my defining moment *as a person* for the rest of my life and it's precisely because of that . . . when people would want to talk about the game I made a real concerted effort to avoid it and I shunned publicity. [At first] I regaled in it for a while and soaked it up as best I could* but after a while it got a little tiring and I didn't want to be remembered

* Not long after the game . . . I believe it was December . . . I got a phone call from a producer at *The Dating Game*. They wanted me to come out and be on the show and they said Brian Dowling was going to be on it also and some other individual who they didn't name at the time—I thought it would be somebody else like . . . maybe one of the coaches—I don't know—maybe one of the coaches was still single. But . . . yeah it was a great experience. I went out to Hollywood and appeared on *The Dating Game* with Brian and, as I recall, I had a good time. Unfortunately neither Brian nor myself won the date. Apparently the gal picked a former boyfriend. I think it was a former boyfriend or someone she had gone out with before . . . and how she could . . . I thought it was rigged. I'm sorry. No offense to *The Dating Game* but she must have recognized his voice. Either that or she didn't like the tone of our voices. She picked the former boyfriend or former date but that was OK because I think they had to go to Hawaii and at that time—as great a place as Hawaii is—I had to go back and do a lot of schoolwork so I didn't really care.

as the unknown who came off the bench and brought the team back, etc., etc. I had this concern and desire to be known for what I was, the person that I was . . . not just for this symbol or what I perceived to be a symbol. So for a number of years after the game I was very protective of myself and my identity, so to speak, and my feelings about the game. I didn't really talk much about it. I didn't want to talk much about it. In fact, I wanted to forget about it.

It's as if, when you were a kid, you rode a bike. You were seven years old and you rode it one day in May for the first time and you shouted *Hallelujah* and your parents loved you for it and the world was great and a wonderful place and fine and dandy, you moved on, you learned to ride the bike . . . but twenty years down the road a friend of yours comes up to you and says, "Hey! Remember the day you learned to ride the bike? How did it feel? It must have been fantastic!" And that's all they want to talk about was that day when you were seven years old and you learned to ride a bike . . . it was seventy-two degrees . . . it was a wonderful sunny day . . . it was a great moment in your life . . . but hey . . . years have passed. You've done other things in your life but that person insisted on talking about that one day in your life when you learned to ride a bike.

That's sort of how I felt: that that was a great moment in my life but it was just *that*—a moment in my life. It wasn't my whole life. I felt very uncomfortable with people looking at me. I felt like a piece of meat, or a symbol. A symbolic piece of meat, I guess. Well, that's the wrong analogy. A symbol. We'll make it less bloody. Less . . . *corporeal*. I just felt like a symbol.

I wanted people to make the effort to get to know me, plain and simple. But as I got older I didn't care any more. You get wiser . . . you realize . . . people are pressed for time . . . I learned to roll with things better. I mellowed with age.

Yale linebacker, Mike Bouscaren: This is a game. This is a ritual that grownups put on young people, partly out of their desire to live through it again, if they ever did the first time, in their children or in younger people . . . to set them up to play this wonderful, ritual contest of life and death and survival. And we didn't know any of that. You know, the coach has got this sign on the wall: "Winning Isn't Everything . . . It's the *Only* Thing." And we're twenty-one years old. We believed that stuff.

In retrospect, people who think back over decades about whether or not this was a facemask call sometimes put themselves back into that position of trying to relive it, trying to correct what happened: *oh no! That was a mistake. We should rewrite . . . do the revisionist rendition of what really happened so that it could happen the way I wanted it to happen in the first place.* But that's not the fact.

The fact is that everyone was out there, twenty-two people on the field at a time, trying to do the best they could . . . not really knowing what it would mean to them later in life.

Harvard cornerback, Rick Frisbie: Mike Bouscaren is another guy who lives in Boston and is a friend of mine and who was a linebacker for Yale. In the early years after this game, when you ran into these guys, it was almost sort of like an inferiority complex. Sort of like *you guys won, 29-29, and we didn't.* And it's like there's a real difference in attitude, that, you know, one guy . . . because of the way the game turned out . . . one guy is successful and the other guy isn't. . . .

Harvard tackle, Fritz Reed: We've got to keep *some* perspective: It was a *football game* . . . and that's *all* it was. It wasn't even for a major championship. It was a great experience. It was both surprising and something to be proud of and to look back on . . . but it was a football game.

Harvard cornerback, Rick Frisbie: . . . when in reality it was just a football game. It had nothing to do, or *shouldn't* have anything to do, with real life that occurs afterwards and it's surprising what kind of effect a game like this can have on someone's life.

Yale linebacker, Mike Bouscaren: Over the years people have asked me, "What did that game mean to you?" and I tell them it was a wonderful character builder. I'm glad that we lost . . . because if we had won I probably would have had more difficulty becoming just a regular person . . . becoming a person who understands that all in life is not fair, that you can't win all the time and it's good to be humble.

Harvard linebacker, Gary Farneti: Student protests and tear gas and women's lib and civil rights . . . they were all converging at the same time. We were growing up in our most formative years in an atmosphere where the entire society was undergoing huge changes across a broad array. Set against that you have an overachieving, smallish, slowish team come back and beat what appeared to be the world champs. I think that summed it up. It was perfectly fitting for the era, that everything's possible. It certainly affected me that way, whether I understood it overtly or subconsciously, that really there are strange things that are possible. You just have to be there ready at the time. I think that's carried through with me. I've heard other of my teammates say it in their adult years. I watched Tommy Lee Jones on an interview show where they asked him . . . they were looking for some turning point in his career . . . and it wasn't a movie . . . he said it was the Harvard-Yale game. It had that type of impact on all of us.

Harvard guard, Tommy Lee Jones: It's a wonderful league to play football in. It really is. I'm very happy about my experience in Harvard football. That was an important part of my life. One of the best things about that day was that my mother and father were able to be there. They came all the way from Ben Gazi, Libya to see the last three or four games that we played my senior year. I'll always be grateful for that.

Yale safety, J.P. Goldsmith: It just changed my life. Yale football . . . I mean the guy could be a bank robber but if he played Yale football he's OK with me. I hope they can preserve it . . . and I don't give a damn if Yale ever goes to the Rose Bowl.

Yale end, Del Marting: When J.P. Goldsmith, for example, looks back on this, or I do, or Dowling does . . . J.P. says this was the best time of our lives and he's right. For me that's true and I'm sure for most of the guys on the team. That was a highlight . . . and that was a moment . . . a way of living and a way of experiencing things that has never been equaled.

Harvard halfback, Ray Hornblower: This was spiritual battle between two great schools and it was divine justice that we ended up tieing because it showed blessings on both our parts. We didn't win. We tied. We both walked away hopefully with our heads pretty high.

Harvard back-up quarterback, Frank Champi: The reality of it is that nobody really lost. I think we all won because as Yale players will say, as they will admit to, and I've heard some of these former ball players have admitted this . . . that if it wasn't for that game they wouldn't be remembered today.

So, by losing—well not losing . . . excuse me . . . sorry about that—by *tieing* . . . by not winning or routing poor Harvard . . . both teams have a small place in football history, especially Ivy League football. So it's a win-win for everybody.

162

WHERE ARE THEY NOW?

Mike Ananis, Harvard cornerback
Andover, Massachusetts
I'm the director of the Rindge School of Technical Arts, which is the career and technical educational component of the Cambridge, Massachusetts public schools.

John Ballantyne, Harvard halfback
Greensboro, North Carolina
I'm in the publishing business. I've been doing that for about thirty years but about four years ago my brother and I launched our own magazine, specific to North Carolina, called "NC Boating Lifestyle."

George Bass, Yale tackle
Williamsburg, Virginia
I'm a professor at The College of William and Mary. I teach educational psychology and topics related to educational research.

Rick Berne, Harvard defensive tackle
Falmouth, Maine
I'm a lawyer.

Mike Bouscaren, Yale linebacker and defensive captain,
Brookline, Massachusetts
I'm involved in the investment world. [Mike Bouscaren runs in ultra-marathons (100-kilometer races). His recent book "Ultrarunning: My Story" explores, among other things, the spiritual side of long distance running.]

Frank Champi, Harvard back-up quarterback
Newburyport, Massachusetts
I've done a variety of things. Mostly I've been in high tech and in an engineering capacity . . . anywhere from doing field service work to being an application engineer. I'm also an inventor. I've got a couple of patents that I've been trying to shop around. One of my patents is a lifting device that attaches to shovels that takes the bending out of lifting. Everybody is complaining about their bad backs . . . well, my device resolves the problem. In fact it solves the problem. If I had a few minutes I'd show you . . . but that's for another time and place. [After the interview Frank Champi did show me his device . . . attached to a snow shovel. It is simple, elegantly designed . . . and it works.]

Andy Coe, Yale linebacker (and future captain - 1969)
Palo Alto, California
I'm director of government and community relations for Stanford Hospital and Clinics.

Pat Conway, Harvard safety
Fairfield, Connecticut

[After Pat Conway graduated from Harvard, The Pittsburgh Steelers (then the worst team in the NFL) expressed interest in him. Not realizing that the Steelers would soon be acquiring a young quarterback named Terry Bradshaw, Conway negotiated himself out of a contract.] I could have had four rings in my future. Or I could have been annihilated. I work as a money manager . . . investment manager . . . in Westport, Connecticut. I have my own firm. We have twenty-five reps. We do investments for 401(k)s, corporations, individuals . . . we run the gamut.

Dr. John Cramer, Harvard defensive end (and future captain - 1969)
Edmonds, Washington

I am a physician. I got a business degree about ten years ago so I do a lot of administrative things and still work as a doctor about a quarter of the time.

Gus Crim, Harvard fullback
Columbus, Ohio

My business career is basically revolved around commercial real estate.

Nick Davidson, Yale halfback
Chino Hills, California

I am a lawyer. I currently own a diagnostic medical center. I specialize in high technology medical businesses and legal problems involving doctors who run them but I'm also involved on the business side. And then I have a ranch, which is a resort . . . a water-ski and wake-boarding resort. That's a place that's all about health and fitness . . . so hopefully that will keep me in shape and enthused. I get a great deal of pleasure from that.

Bob Dowd, Harvard tackle
Dallas, Texas

I am a tax attorney. I deal in litigation with the IRS and tax planning for individuals.

Brian Dowling, Yale captain and quarterback
Burlington, Massachusetts

I spent ten years playing professional football. [Most notably with The New England Patriots.] Since then I've done sales and marketing jobs. I was the executive director of a museum for a number of years. I've worked in non-profits. I've worked for the government. I've worn a lot of hats.

John Emery, Harvard linebacker and defensive captain
Bedford, New Hampshire

I'm a district court judge. I got out of college, taught high school for a year, did some coaching . . . coached high school sports during that year. Then I went to law school, became a lawyer. I've been a lawyer since 1973. I was appointed in 2001 as a judge.

Gary Farneti, Harvard linebacker (and future captain - 1970)
Binghamton, New York

I'm an attorney and a partner in the firm of Levine, Gouldin and Thompson. I'm a trial attorney . . . basically civil litigation.

Bruce Freeman, Harvard end
Bakersfield, California

I am the president of a company called Castle and Cooke. We do master plan communities and commercial developments all over the United States.

Rick Frisbie, Harvard cornerback
Boston, Massachusetts

I'm in the venture capital business, having started a firm with two other partners back in 1983, so I've been at it for almost twenty-five years.

Fran Gallagher, Yale defensive tackle
North Olmsted, Ohio

I'm an attorney. I have my own company that does third party administration of companies' qualified retirement plans, 401(k) plans and things of that nature.

Jim Gallagher, Yale defensive end
North Royalton, Ohio

I'm an attorney, a public defender mostly, over at Parma Court. I do pretty much all criminal defense trial work.

Vic Gatto, Harvard captain and halfback
Canton, Massachusetts

I've had a many-varied career. I spent twenty-five years coaching college football at Bates College in Lewiston, Maine; Tufts University in Medford, Massachusetts and then down at Davidson College in Davidson, North Carolina. I was committed to coaching at great academic institutions where football was *not* the most important thing in the kids' lives and really had, I think, a wonderful career. We had excellent teams . . . All-American players in some cases . . . some undefeated teams . . . so it was a really good career. I went from there into the environmental business and also the education business. I got a doctorate in education and currently have a company that does educational networking for school districts that can't afford it. We build large-scale high bandwidth networks for inner-city schools . . . Springfield, Massachusetts, for example . . . Somerville, Massachusetts . . . and many other school districts, including New Haven . . . where we give them the opportunity to bring in educational content in a way that wealthy school districts do routinely. So that's one business that I do. I also have a renewable energy business that builds power plants using biomass fuel. We're doing that in Springfield, Massachusetts . . . Erie, Pennsylvania and down in Rhode Island. So we've got a couple of things going on and at this point in my career I'm fortunate enough to be able to do things that I think matter and have the good experience of helping people in some ways in dealing with issues of education equity and also the issues of renewable energy . . . so . . . it's a lot of fun.

Kyle Gee, Yale tackle
Piedmont, California.

I do appellate law. I read transcripts and write briefs and go to court about five or six times a year.

J.P. Goldsmith, Yale safety
Lexington, Massachusetts

I am an institutional salesman for Lehman Brothers. I've been doing that for ten years and before that I worked for a firm that no longer exists . . . a part of Citigroup . . . called Solomon Brothers. [The interview was conducted in 2007. Since then, Lehman Brothers has ceased to exist. J.P. Goldsmith is now an institutional salesman for Barclays Capital.]

Pete Hall, Harvard defensive end
Wellesley, Massachusetts
I'm just recently retired. I was a high school teacher for thirteen years and then I left and went into business in the financial services area. My expertise was in sales and marketing. I'm semi-retired. I do a little consulting. I umpire college baseball.

Ray Hornblower, Harvard halfback
New York City, New York
I still sing professionally. I sang professionally for about twenty-five years in opera houses in Europe and California and about four years ago I decided I had to start thinking about my retirement fund so I do help early stage health care technologists develop technologies that hopefully will save lives. [Before becoming an opera singer Hornblower was a lawyer in the Civil Rights Division of the Justice Department.]

Neil Hurley, Harvard cornerback
Winchester, Massachusetts
I am in commercial real estate. I do build-outs and manage construction projects.

John Ignacio, Harvard cornerback
San Francisco, California
I'm a school administrator in the San Francisco Unified School District.

Bob Jannino, Harvard guard
Stamford, Connecticut
I do a couple of different things. I'm the president of a company called Office Power, which installs co-generation devices in office buildings. We own the power plants that we put in these buildings. It's a concept that today is in sync with what the regulatory authorities are trying to do and it's in sync with the whole concept of carbon footprints and reducing uses of fossil fuels or at least using it more efficiently. The second thing that I do is work with a guy who is a Harvard grad . . . I think he graduated in 1980 . . . a guy named Jonathon Garrity who created a company called Cambridge Hanover, which is an investment advisory arm on the real estate side. We acquire industrial buildings.

Tommy Lee Jones, Harvard guard
San Antonio, Texas
[Tommy Lee Jones is an Academy Award winning film actor. He once said, "I love cinema and I love agriculture." An avid horseman, he owns and operates a cattle ranch near San Antonio where he hosts the Harvard polo team each fall.]

Lonny Kaplan, Harvard defensive tackle
Princeton, New Jersey
I'm a lawyer. I have a small law firm in Trenton . . . trial practice.

Ron Kell, Yale monster back
Mill Valley, California
I'm in the mortgage banking business. I actually spent several years as a member of the Pacific Stock Exchange and now I've moved on to something a little less stressful.

Bill Kelly, Harvard defensive back
Needham, Massachusetts
I'm a residential mortgage banker.

John Kiernan, Harvard end
Milton, Massachusetts

I'm a lawyer. I have a law firm that's in eight states and the District of Columbia, so I travel a bit. It's civil law. It's all litigation, primarily on the defense side. We dabble a little bit in criminal defense. We have a number of former prosecutors, as I am, so that still holds interest for me . . . but primarily it's civil . . . a defense firm.

Mick Kleber, Yale defensive tackle
Valley Village, California

I'm an independent writer and producer . . . mostly of special content for the motion picture business. I have a large experience in music videos as well. I'm the son of two military people. My mother was a WAVE during the war. My father was a Marine officer for his entire life . . . from Iwo Jima through three tours in Vietnam. So it was kind of logical for me to be in the NROTC. I had a scholarship to Yale. I went into the Marines myself. I was a platoon commander in Vietnam, a White House aide [under Nixon] and a Marine Corps representative to the Bicentennial Committee. Then I resigned my commission when I was a captain, came to California and became one of the original music video execu-tives for Capital Records back in 1980. After a thirteen year run there . . . over seven hundred videos . . . I went into business for myself. And in 1999 I went into a venture called Spotlight Health where I started doing celebrity-driven health cam-paigns. I did that for six years and then just recently here now I've come back to the movie thing and I'm writing a feature film for Dimension Films [the Weinstein brothers].

President Nixon, Mick Kleber and Mamie Eisenhower.

George Lalich, Harvard quarterback
Boulder City, Nevada

[Originally from Chicago where his father was a prizefighter, George Lalich now lives near Las Vegas. He is a lawyer, specializing in horse racing and gaming.]

Brad Lee, Yale guard
Canton, Massachusetts

I'm a professor for the U.S. military . . . Professor of Strategy at the Naval War College in Newport, Rhode Island.

KR: *Now usually at this point in the interview I move on but I have to confess that I'm really interested in what you do.*

BL: Right. I figured someone who made a film called *The Atomic Café* probably would be.

KR: *Can you tell me a little bit more about what it is?*

BL: Basically, we teach a course to mid-career and senior military officers, American and foreign, and also government officials...on how to win wars and secure the peace.

KR: *How did you get into this line of work?*

BL: Well, actually I was a professor of history at Harvard . . . I'm sure the only per-son who played in that game who ended up on the Harvard faculty . . . and I taught there for about eight years and I didn't get tenure. I was looking for something else to do. I knew I didn't want to do history anymore. I was just about to take an appointment teaching a required first year course at the Business School across the river, or perhaps going into money management, outside of academia complete-ly, and I got asked to go down to Newport. I had just written my first piece on a military subject. I went down and gave a presentation. They didn't like it. I got back home to Boston that night. The phone rang. It was the chairman of the Strategy Department there. He said, "How would you like to come to Newport to teach strategy?" I said "Strategy? I don't know anything about strategy." He said, "It doesn't matter. You'll learn." It just sort of struck my fancy. I went intending to stay a year or two. They didn't fire me. I liked it. I've been there twenty years now.

KR: *I'm just wondering . . . because it's guys like you who are teaching our military . . . the number one military power in the history of the world, probably . . . how to do their job. And here you go down there and you didn't know anything about it. What was it about you that made this guy want to hire you to do this?*

BL: We teach in political/military teams so we have a civilian who has been a high level government official, or an academic, and we all get paired with a military officer and we teach jointly. So in twenty years you learn quite a bit. Military officers work through the ranks. They know how to lead people in battle. They know how to operate weapons systems. But strategy . . . war . . . is much bigger than just the shooting.

KR: *So you came in on the political side . . . the historical/political side.*

BL: I did. And we do it through case studies . . . some going way back to the ancient Greeks and some of it is ongoing stuff. We do quite a bit about what's going on in Iraq, Afghanistan, Iran, North Korea . . . so we cover the waterfront.

KR: *Look, I have to ask you this. Did they ask you what you thought about invading Iraq?*

BL: No. That's above my pay grade.

Bob Levin, Yale fullback
Highland Park, Illinois

I'm a teacher, a psychologist. I work with special-needs kids and I've been doing that now for the last thirty-eight years, currently at New Trier High School, which is a local high school just down the road [in Winnetka, Illinois]. I've been coaching football as well, keeping my hand in the game. It's a wonderful diversion for me to be with really healthy kids, at least part of the day.

Ted Livingston, Yale tackle
Brookline, Massachusetts

I'm currently the director of the Massachusetts 9/11 Fund, which is a charitable organization related to the events of September 11, 2001.

Alex MacLean, Harvard middle guard
Lincoln, Massachusetts

I'm an aerial photographer. I fly . . . and photograph . . . myself . . . solo, in the plane.

KR: *So how does that work? Do you have the cameras built in?*

AM: No. It's hand held.

KR: *You fly the airplane with one hand and take the pictures with the other?*

AM: Well, you fly with your feet. You can trim the plane so it flies straight and level and then you have your feet on the rudder so you can make adjustments.

KR: *How did you get into that?*

AM: I learned how to fly in architecture school. I started using it for site analysis and personal expression fine art. So it's been a good run. It's fun. I do a lot of interesting projects. I work with a lot of different people . . . architects, planners, environmentalists . . . I'm working on a project now on climate change.

KR: *Have you ever had any close calls?*

AM: More close calls with the FAA than with falling out of the sky.

Pat Madden, Yale defensive end,
Woodridge, Connecticut

I work currently for Merrill Lynch . . . for their trust company. [Pat Madden has since retired].

Jerry Marino, Harvard linebacker
San Diego, California

I'm what's called a performance technologist or an instructional systems designer. I work on learning training and performance projects programs.

Del Marting, Yale End
Reno, Nevada

I spent three and a half years in the Navy with Seal Team 2 in Little Creek, Virginia. Following that I went to Harvard Business School for two years . . . graduated in '75. Then I joined Amax, Inc., a mining company based in Greenwich [Connecticut] and I lived there and worked there for about ten years. At the end of my period at Amax I was stationed in France and I ran the European office as chief financial officer for Amax. Following that I bought a mining company here in Reno, which is why I ended up locating here. It was a gold mine, which we sold to a large New Mexico utility and that kind of launched me into a number of venture capital transactions involving aerospace. I worked with Hughes Aircraft in L.A. for a number of years. Recently I've been doing my own deals in the venture world . . . things like biotech in the diabetes area and other miscellaneous types of ventures.

Rich Mattas, Yale tackle
Elizabeth, Illinois

My profession was nuclear science and energy research and I spent most of that time studying fusion. After graduate school I ended up at Argonne National Laboratory, which is one of the major national labs coming out of the Manhattan Project. It's outside of Chicago. Their expertise is really nuclear energy research and that's where nuclear reactors were developed. About the time that I got involved, which was the mid-'70s, fusion research was really taking off. So I had an opportunity to get involved. Luckily I've been able to pursue that for about twenty-five years. I've been able to work with some of the best nuclear scientists in the world over that time. Right now I'm retired and I'm living in a great part of the country and enjoying it very much.

Joe McKinney, Harvard defensive end
Spring Branch, Texas

I've been a banker for thirty-four years. I was chairman and CEO of J.P. Morgan Chase Bank in San Antonio until I retired. I stayed retired for about six months and then went back to a small community-owned bank called Broadway Bank where I am the vice-chairman.

Fred Morris, Yale center
Minneapolis, Minnesota

I'm a lawyer. When I graduated from Yale I went in as a Vista volunteer in Kansas City, in the inner city, and basically hung out with . . . for lack of a better word — it was a pretty unstructured existence — with a black street gang and had really an incredible experience with those guys. In fact my youngest son Andy is named after one of those gang members who I thought was just a wonderful human being . . . who ended up in Leavenworth . . . but . . . he was a wonderful human being and in any other circumstance I think he could have been a really productive member of society. I think the practice of law is . . . there's a lot of bullshit in the practice of law and I have . . . particularly in litigation I can be a pretty adept bullshitter. So I've been pretty successful at it . . . but, you know, I don't take it all that seriously. The page turns and nobody knows that some case has been resolved and finished and you go on to the next one.

Dale Neal, Harvard linebacker
Pacific Palisades, California

[Dale Neal is now a semi-retired lawyer specializing in real estate and land use.]

Tom Neville, Yale defensive tackle (and future captain - 1970)
Incline Village, Nevada

I got drafted by the Colts . . . but I wasn't thrilled by some of the experiences I had heard about from some of the older guys. I got a Rhodes Scholarship and elected to go to England. I read politics and economics at Oxford for two years. I was fortunate enough to play rugby, which I had never done, for Oxford and was in two of the varsity matches against Cambridge including the centenary match where I had the interesting privilege to shake hands with Queen Elizabeth in her steel-gloved hand and Prince Philip, who wanted to know why my hair was so long and whether they pulled it in the scrum. I said, "They wouldn't dare." I went to Stanford, got a Ph.D and started a consulting firm that ended up working for the federal government. I was one of the first hires in the Carter Administration's Department of Energy and did a lot of international security and deregulation stuff. I went to an energy shipping company in San Francisco. I got into industrial combustion where I've helped build a significant international engineering company and some important ultra-low emissions patents based on my inventions. Now I am developing a system called Dynamic Screening for prostate cancer, which looks at biomarkers over time. It's proving to be a really promising success. It opens up a field called Computational Diagnostics and will eventually be applied to most cancers. It's really exciting and we're working with some of the top guys in the world right now to bring this to market.

Tom Peacock, Yale tackle
Media, Pennsylvania

I work for Wyeth. Wyeth is a pharmaceutical manufacturer. I've been in the pharmaceutical business for almost twenty years now. Prior to that I worked for NFL Films.

Jack Perkowski, Yale guard
Beijing, China and Lambertville, New Jersey

KR: You were an American Studies major at Yale. Now I understand that you are a manufacturer and distributor of automotive parts in The People's Republic of China. Could you briefly tell me how you got from one place to the next?

JP: Well, that's a question a lot of people ask. They say, "Jack, I can kind of trace the line from Pittsburgh to Yale to Harvard Business School . . . " And then I worked on Wall St. for twenty years. I ran the investment banking business at Paine Webber. But then people say, "I can't quite make the connection between Paine Webber and Wall St. . . . and China." But very simply in 1990, after a twenty-year career on Wall St., I decided I wanted to do something completely different for a second career. I wanted to find a long-term trend and then put an organization together to get out ahead of that trend. I basically decided to look at Asia. I was interested in Asia because Asia has half the world's population with an average age in the low twenties and that meant that those Asian economies were going to continue to grow into the 21st Century and I thought that would be one of the biggest opportunities to come along in a long time. I made my first trip to Hong Kong at the end of '91 and started to focus on China in '92. We're actually not a distributor. We distribute automotive parts but we're a manufacturer. So we have eighteen factories now in China . . . twelve thousand employees. We're one of the largest manufacturers of components in China. But that's roughly how I got from Pittsburgh, Yale, Harvard, Wall St. . . . .to China.

KR: Can you tell me what the experience of doing business in China is like these days?

JP: Oh, it's just a fantastic experience. As I tell people, there's never been a country as large as China going through what it's going through in such a short period of time. To be part of that, in some small way, is one of the most exciting things I've done in my entire life. It's just absolutely fascinating. The country is massive in terms of size. It's massive in terms of people. It's got a population that is very much anxious to catch up on a lot of lost time. The pace is very fast. The country changes constantly. [Jack Perkowski has written a book: *Managing the Dragon: How I'm building a Billion Dollar Business in China.* (Published by Random House . . . Crown Business)]

Milton Puryear, Yale middle guard
Brooklyn, New York

I'm the principal planner for the Brooklyn Waterfront Greenway, which is a four-teen-mile continuous bike/pedestrian linear park along the Brooklyn waterfront that will connect other parks. I also have a contract to create and work on a park and greenway in Stamford, Connecticut. Prior to that I was an investment analyst. I've been an investment banker. I've still got some entrepreneurial things going on in the background . . . but that's what I do.

KR: Did you have some sort of environmental epiphany that caused you to switch careers?

MP: No. The biggest epiphany for me, I guess, was that I bought bicycles for my wife and daughter . . . my young daughter at the time . . . and after riding across the Brooklyn Bridge once, my daughter told me, "I don't want to ride on the streets of New York any more. It's too scary." It made me think of what it means to be a kid . . . to be able to take your bike out and go and ride . . . that freedom that New York kids just don't have. It's just not a viable option. But if there were a safe place where people could ride and kids could ride where they would just have to cross one street or so . . . then that would be a nice thing. That would be something we could do for our kids. That was one part of my inspiration.

Dr. Steve Ranere, Harvard defensive end
Belmont, Massachusetts

I went to Tufts Medical School, trained in Boston with a short stint out in San Francisco . . . and started a medical group here thirty years ago with my partner. We've grown that to a twenty-something person group.

Fritz Reed, Harvard tackle
Powell, Ohio

I'm now, I'm sort of in a third career...I'm a consultant with a consulting group out of Chicago that runs insolvent companies. I was for twenty-five years a bankrupt-cy lawyer and then I spent five years as the chief financial officer of Wendy's International and now I'm doing something that's sort of halfway between those two. [Fritz Reed died, suddenly, shortly after the interview, in 2007.]

Jim Reynolds, Harvard halfback
Short Hills, New Jersey

I work in Summit, New Jersey. I have my own consulting firm, The Reynolds Financial Services Group. It's basically a financial due-diligence firm in the mort-gage finance arena. We do a lot of work for banks and Wall Street mortgage finance companies.

Scott Robinson, Yale defensive end
Vail, Colorado (at the time of the interview)
Corona Del Mar, California (currently)

I work in insurance.

Gary Singleterry, Harvard punter
Plainfield, New Jersey

I'm on my second career. I manage a small hedge fund and I've got some other money under management for a couple of corporate accounts. It's a fund that spe-cializes in mortgage-backed securities . . . nothing terribly exciting. [!] I've been doing that for a little over ten years. My first career was as an investment banker in New York City. That's a young man's business and so I gave that up about twelve, fifteen years ago. I'm managing money and having a lot of fun doing it . . . with an office here in Summit, New Jersey.

Ted Skowronski, Harvard center
Southbury, Connecticut.

[Ted Skowronski is a civil litigation attorney.]

Dr. Ken Thomas, defensive back (and onside kick specialist)
Bedford, New Hampshire.
I'm a physician . . . internal medicine...but primary care these days.

Pete Varney, Harvard end
Acton, Massachusetts
Immediately after Harvard I played professional baseball for seven years. I got a proverbial "cup of coffee" and played maybe two and a half years in the big leagues [as a catcher with the Chicago White Sox]. I went on and taught at Narragansett Regional High School. I coached three sports: football, basketball and baseball. In 1982 I got the job of baseball coach here at Brandeis and I've been here ever since.

Dr. John Waldman, Yale cornerback
Slingerlands, New York
I am a pediatric neurosurgeon. I'm full time faculty at Albany Medical College. I'm a professor . . . teach . . . practice, etc.

Bruce Weinstein, Yale end
Southbury, Connecticut
When I first left college I had aspirations of becoming a professional football player and played for the balance of the season with the Bridgeport Jets, the New York Jets farm team, after I was drafted and cut by Miami and got a tryout in Denver and didn't make it there either. After that I bounced around with a number of jobs including the New York City Department of Consumer Affairs . . . I was a substitute teacher . . . I worked on a tugboat . . . I went car racing . . . and eventually wound up at Exxon Enterprises, a new venture arm of Exxon. That brought me to Connecticut. I got involved with a former teammate in the real estate syndication business and I think whatever I've done in the last twenty years has been related to that.

Dick Williams, Yale middle guard
Wilmington, North Carolina
I am chief counsel for Global Nuclear Fuel, which is a unit of General Electric.

Tom Wynne, Harvard safety
Fordyce, Arkansas
I started practicing law [in 1976] here in Fordyce at my family law firm with my father and uncle. They are both deceased now and I'm practicing law here in Fordyce with my brother Robin, my youngest brother, who was the Harvard class of '75. So I've been practicing law now for over thirty years . . . right here in Fordyce. It's a private practice. It's a family law practice. It's actually the firm that my grandfather founded almost a hundred years ago. He practiced until 1934 and passed away and then my uncle Frank came back in about 1950 and re-founded the firm and then he and Dad practiced until . . . Dad passed away in '87 . . . Frank died in '80. At one point there were four of us. It's just a small town family law practice. We do domestic relations . . . personal injury . . . all of us have been prosecuting attorneys . . . I've been a mayor. My brother Robin right now is the District Judge . . . sort of a traffic judge . . . as was my father . . . my uncle was the prosecuting attorney for many years . . . as was I . . . so, you know, when you practice law in a small town like Fordyce, Dallas County, Arkansas, you wear a lot of hats.

ACKNOWLEDGMENTS

Sincere thanks go to: Garry Trudeau for his splendid generosity in allowing the use of his *Bull Tales* comic strips; Harvard Athletic Director Robert Scalise and WHDH-TV General Manager Michael Carson for providing access to the broadcast of the game; the late, great sportscaster Don Gillis for his sparkling play-by-play commentary and to his widow Kathy McGarry-Gillis and son Gary Gillis for letting me use it; my former Harvard film teacher Robert Gardner, Sue Bodine, Karen Cooper and Thom Powers for being early champions of the film which is the basis of this book; Matt Glasser for his deft transcription of the interviews; my friend Mark Michaelson for selflessly sharing his awesome artistic talent at key moments in this project; my oldest friend Derek Huntington for support in many forms; Martin Burga for guiding me gently into the world of computer graphics; layout artist Bernie Schleifer for his talent, patience and professionalism; and my editor Aaron Schlechter who had the questionable insight to make a deal with a stranger in a bar based on overheard ramblings.

My deepest gratitude goes to the sixty-one former football players who welcomed me warmly on my travels around the country and shared their stories with passion and eloquence.